The Catholic Handbook for
Visiting the Sick
and Homebound

2009
Year B

LTP
LITURGY
TRAINING
PUBLICATIONS

Nihil Obstat
D. Todd Williamson
Censor Deputatus
April 24, 2008

Imprimatur
Reverend John F. Canary, STL, DMin.
Vicar General
Archdiocese of Chicago
April 25, 2008

Concordat cum originali
Monsignor Anthony F. Sherman
Executive Director
USCCB Secretariat of Divine Worship

TABLE OF CONTENTS

[Lectionary Readings are from Year B. Please note that during Lent, the scrutiny readings for Year A are not provided.]

The Gospel and Explanation of the Reading

Advent

Christmas

Ordinary Time I

Lent

Easter

INTRODUCTION

Come to me, all you who labor and are burdened,
and I will give you rest. Take my yoke upon you and
learn from me, for I am meek and humble of heart;
and you will find rest for yourselves. For my yoke is
easy, and my burden light.

—Matthew 11:28

Suffering wears a thousand faces, and every face is Christ's. When we suffer sickness, loss, violence, or the harsher effects of aging in ourselves or in those we love, we cannot really understand the reasons, but we can choose the rock on which to stand. We are members of the Body of Christ. Christ our Head becomes present in our suffering; in our dying we share his death; his voyage through death to the glory of the Resurrection becomes our journey. In him, we are held securely in the face of the anxiety, fear, anger, guilt, and grief that sickness, aging, or suffering can bring.

One of the deepest causes of suffering experienced by those whom sickness or aging confines to the narrow world of home, hospital, or geriatric facility is a sense of isolation. We may feel misunderstood, rejected, abandoned by the healthy world of which we were a part, even by those who love us, even by God. There is something wrong with us. We are no longer useful. We cause other people discomfort and inconvenience. We may know how we "ought" to pray in times of suffering, but we can't seem to do it. We can't even go to church.

When we have suffered traumatic loss or violence, we may suffer a similar sense of loneliness. Our experience has set us apart. We may feel that no one can understand what we have endured. We find ourselves unable to take an interest in the world of everyday concerns about which others are busy. We may even find ourselves ill at ease with our ordinary companions in faith and worship. Our usual forms of prayer no longer seem to suffice. We have questions that are difficult to answer: Why me? Why has God allowed this to happen? We may be angry with God *and* ashamed of our anger. On the other hand, we may find ourselves more deeply in communion with the suffering Christ or with his bereaved and sorrowful Mother than before yet separated from others by the intensity of our spiritual experience.

Ministers of Care, both the laity and the ordained, are sent to step across the moat that isolates the sufferers, bringing them the comfort of personal presence and prayer. Ministries of care are as diverse as the parishes that sponsor them. Some parishes may have full-time lay pastoral associates or other employees who specialize in pastoral care. These lay people may have been specially trained, participating in pastoral care internships (Clinical Pastoral Education), or receiving undergraduate or graduate degrees in pastoral care or diocesan or national certification. Parishes also may be fortunate to have volunteers who provide pastoral care to those in hospitals, hospices, nursing homes, prisons, police stations, crisis centers, and to those who are dying or have lost a loved one. These volunteers can provide music, proclaim scripture, offer words of consolation and hope, or simply silent presence.

The most familiar ministry of care is that of Extraordinary Minister of Holy Communion. The word *extraordinary* can be confusing. In this case, the Church uses it officially to distinguish between ordained bishops, priests, and deacons, who are the *ordinary* ministers of Holy Communion, and specially commissioned lay people who fill the gaps, so to speak, when there are not enough ordinary ministers to give Holy Communion to everyone at Mass or to take Holy Communion to the sick and the homebound. The words *extraordinary* and *ordinary* as they are used here may seem odd because they recall a time when there were so many priests that there was no need for lay people to take on this role.

This handbook is specially designed for the use of *lay* Ministers of Care, so it does *not* contain the rites for the sacraments of Penance or the Anointing of the Sick, or the special prayers and blessings used by ordained bishops, priests, or deacons. All lay ministers who provide care to those who are sick, homebound, isolated, or suffering in some way will benefit from the contents of this book.

You, as a Minister of Care, have been called to be a sign and a bridge. Sent by the parish, you are the living witness that the community of faith and worship has not forgotten the absent sick, the invisible elderly, and the unseen sufferers. Praying with them as a representative of Christ living in the Church, you are a sign that God is and wants to be with them. You draw them back into conscious communion with the whole Body of Christ. They, and in many cases their caregivers, are not alone.

The Church has provided two official books which contain a wealth of rites for those who visit, pray with, or bring Holy Communion to the sick, aging, dying, or others who are struggling with addiction, personal violence, or the loss of a child through miscarriage—especially those cut off from fully participating in the liturgical life of their local Church or parish. These ritual books are called *Pastoral Care of the Sick: Rites of Anointing and Viaticum* and the *Book of Blessings*. *Pastoral Care of the Sick* contains rites specific to those who are sick and dying, providing orders of prayer for the sacraments of Eucharist, Penance, and Anointing of the Sick. The *Book of Blessings* provides multiple orders of blessing for various needs and occasions. What you have in your hand, *The Catholic Handbook for Visiting the Sick and Homebound 2009*, is a booklet containing all of the rituals from *Pastoral Care of the Sick* and the *Book of Blessings* that can be used by lay people when visiting the sick and the homebound. Everything you will need is right here! You will be able to use this book when you are sent to give Holy Communion to other parishioners or pray with: those who are confined to their homes, to hospitals, or to geriatric centers; those who have suffered the traumatic loss of a child through miscarriage; those who suffer from addictions; and those who have been victims of violence. The most important resource you have as a minister, though, is your personal relationship with Christ, our healer and our Savior. You too are the face of Christ.

USING THIS BOOK

The Catholic Handbook for Visiting the Sick and Homebound 2009 will tell you what the Church asks of you, as her spokesperson, to say and do when you visit, pray with, or give Holy Communion to those who suffer. You need not worry about making up prayers—they are provided here for you! In fact, *except* where the rite itself calls for adaptation, you must use the prayers as they are written because they express the common faith of the Catholic Church to which we all committed ourselves in Baptism. We are called to help one another to grow into the full breadth and depth of that faith. When you pray in the name of the Church you represent, you are asking the sick and others who gather with them to say "Amen," that is, "Yes, I agree, I will abide by that, and I want God to do what you are asking in our name." The Church is very clear that "no one has the authority to add, remove, or change anything in the liturgy" (*Constitution on the Sacred Liturgy*, 22.2).

CONTENTS OF THIS BOOK

You, as a Minister of Care, will be called upon to offer those whom you visit an opportunity to benefit from the strengthening power of prayer by making use of one many rites and orders of prayer and blessing provided by the Church. This book contains everything you will need to give Holy Communion and other rites for praying with the sick and others who suffer for various reasons. The rites and prayers are divided into three sections:

- Section 1: Blessings of and Visits to the Sick and Suffering
- Section 2: Holy Communion
- Section 3: Pastoral Care of the Dying

Each of these sections contains the official rites and orders of prayer as provided by the Church in both the *Book of Blessings* and *Pastoral Care of the Sick: Rites of Anointing and Viaticum*. The following notes will help you navigate these rites.

BLESSINGS OF AND VISITS TO THE SICK AND SUFFERING

Visiting and Blessing the Sick: You may be sent to visit the sick simply to pray with them. However, sometimes you may be prepared to give Holy Communion, but you discover that those you are visiting are unable to receive for some reason. At still other times, you may be visiting Catholic patients in an institution, but others who are not Catholic recognize you as a minister and ask you to pray with them. You need not turn away, feeling that you have nothing to offer. These are just a few of the situations when you could use these rites for visiting the sick and the suffering—either to prepare them to receive Holy Communion during a later visit or simply to enable them to draw strength and comfort from the healing presence of Christ who has promised to be there whenever two or three gather in his name (see Matthew 18:20).

Titles of these rites: Some clarification about the titles of the services contained in this book is needed to prevent confusion. The book entitled *Pastoral Care of the Sick: Rites of Anointing and Viaticum* provides two rites for visiting the sick: "Visits to the Sick" and "Visits to a Sick Child." "Visits to the Sick" is used with adults. The *Book of Blessings* also provides two rites entitled "Order for the Blessing of Adults" and "Order for the Blessing of Children." Here the word "order" simply means "order of service." These two "orders" presents an entire service of optional song, scripture, prayer, and blessing. The two rites from *Pastoral Care of the Sick* are simple prayers for visiting the sick.

The Liturgies: The "Orders for the Blessing of the Sick" (see pages 22–61) begin with a simple sign of the cross and invitation to pray followed by a reading of the Word of God whereas "Visits to the Sick" (see pages 66–79) begin with the reading. "Visits to the Sick" continues with the Lord's Prayer and a choice of concluding prayers designed to address some of the different circumstances in which the sick might find themselves. For example, concluding prayer option A references those who "suffer pain, illness or disease"; option B pleas for the sick to be restored to health; and option C requests that the sick may find "peace of mind." Consider your options in relation to the situation of the person you are visiting. If you happen to be visiting someone who isn't Catholic, you may use this order of service, but remember to remind them tactfully that Catholics end the Lord's Prayer after "deliver us from evil." If not, be prepared for them to add the longer ending, "for thine is the kingdom, the power and the glory" before the "Amen." Above all, you do not want to cause distress to anyone.

In the "Orders for Blessing of the Sick" the Word of God may be followed with an explanation of the reading then a litany of intercession. The Church urges the minister to encourage the sick to participate in Christ's redemptive work by uniting their sufferings to his and by praying for the needs of the world. Prayer for others is an effective antidote to the self-preoccupation to which sickness and aging can tempt us. Intercessions provide an excellent way of meeting this need. You may allow participants the opportunity to add petitions of their own, but beware of causing embarrassment by prolonging the silence if it becomes clear that they have nothing to say.

Both the rites for "Visits to the Sick" and "Orders for the Blessing of the Sick" end with prayers of blessing which may be said over the person who is ill. The "Orders for the Blessing of the Sick" provides two prayers of blessing. The first option is for more than one person, whereas the second option is for a single individual. The rite stipulates that the minister is to make the sign of the cross on the forehead of the sick while saying the prayer. The gesture may be unexpected or unfamiliar, especially coming from a lay minister, so it is wise to let people know what you are preparing to do. This may be followed with a prayer for the protection of the Blessed Virgin Mary. The rite suggests singing a familiar Marian song, such as *Hail, Holy Queen Enthroned Above*. If music is unavailable, only sing if those you are visiting are able to participate. See also "Music Preparations" on page 14.

"Orders for the Blessing of the Sick" and "Visits to the Sick" end with a concluding prayer. In both rites, the "lay minister invokes the Lord's blessing on the sick and all present by signing himself or herself with the sign of the cross."

"Visits to the Sick" includes two prayers of blessing: one for a sick person and one for the elderly. Please note that the lay minister does not make the same gesture as given in "Orders for the Blessing of the Sick." Simply say the prayer.

The "Order for the Blessing of Children" (page 31) and "Visits to a Sick Child" (page 75) follow the same pattern as those used for adults, but they use simpler language. You will have to decide which rite or order of blessing is appropriate to use with older children. A word of caution: Before you make the sign of the cross on the child's head during the blessing, it would be wise to alert parents or caregivers to see if they have any objections. It is also wise to explain this to the child. Remember that very sick children may have experienced unpleasant medical procedures and may fear the unexplained touch of an unfamiliar adult.

Visiting and Blessing those who Suffer: In addition to the rites for visiting and blessing the sick, the *Catholic Handbook* contains three additional services for blessing those who suffer and may not be able to participate in Sunday Eucharist:

- Blessing a Person Suffering from Addiction or from Substance Abuse
- Blessing a Victim of Crime or Oppression
- Blessing Parents after a Miscarriage

If you visit the sick, you may meet people in need of one of these special blessings. You may meet them in a health care setting. For example, a patient may have been hospitalized as a result of addictive behavior or alcohol and drug abuse. Sometimes you may meet a patient who has suffered personal violence, such as domestic abuse, rape, a drive-by shooting, injuries sustained in an accident caused by a drunk driver, injuries sustained at the hands of those engaged in criminal activities, such as robbery, or a person afflicted from post-traumatic stress disorder. You may also find that a woman has suffered a miscarriage, and she and the father are grieving together. You may also find people among the families of those you are visiting to pray with them or give them Holy Communion at home or in an institutional environment. An elderly person might indicate a child or grandchild who is suffering one of these needs and ask you to pray with them. You may be among those assigned to special ministries of care in settings such as support groups.

Be aware that the reason for the need may be recent or long-standing. Sometimes, someone who is coping with illness, confinement in a geriatric facility, or other situation which has brought you to them will want to discuss something that happened long ago and continues to haunt them. Periods of inactivity brought on by sickness or aging give us plenty of time to think and may spur us to make peace with the past in a new way. These orders of blessing offer that opportunity.

Whenever you meet someone in one of these situations, you may use the appropriate order of blessing from the pages that follow. All of them follow the same pattern: an opening rite (sign of the cross, simple greeting, optional introduction), reading and response, including the opportunity to comment on the reading, intercessions, the Lord's Prayer, a prayer of blessing directed to the particular needs of participants, and a concluding rite (general blessing). The Church encourages adaptation, provided the order of service is followed and the major elements included. For example, you might want to personalize the opening introduction, following the general pattern of the one provided here. Here is one example of a personalized introduction to the "Order for Blessing a Victim of Crime or Oppression." Imagine that you are praying with and for a young woman who is a victim of date rape. You might say something like this:

"God has always shown care and compassion for people who have suffered acts of violence, like the one that has brought you here. We commend you, [use the woman's name], to God, who binds up all our wounds, heals us from the pain of betrayal, and restores us to our rightful dignity as a child of God."

The introduction now refers to the victim's own experience, uses her name, and avoids language that could summon up frightening images of being held by a male person.

You will want to choose those intercessions that are most appropriate. You may invite participants to add their own and you may also do so. Turning one's own suffering into prayer for others is both a way of uniting oneself with the redemptive suffering of Christ and turning one's attention outward. If you are accustomed to using the "Orders for Blessing of the Sick," please note that there are some differences between them and these orders of blessing for those otherwise in distress. In particular, these latter orders call for the Lord's Prayer, which often provides the comfort of a familiar prayer; and they do *not* call for the minister to touch the person while saying the prayer of blessing for them. This can be an important courtesy when using this order for blessing with those who have suffered personal violence and shy away from being touched by strangers, even in prayers of blessing.

Like the "Orders for the Blessing of the Sick," these orders also provide a shorter form: a short invitation to prayer, a short reading, and a prayer of blessing. These short forms are particularly useful when ministering to those who have very recently experienced a crisis in addiction, an incident of violence, or a miscarriage, and are too distressed to concentrate on a longer ritual. They are also helpful when you are visiting the person for some other reason and find a need to help them deal with one of these issues.

One of the hidden benefits of the Church's rites of prayer is that they teach us to think in harmony with the Church. If you have never experienced the particular need for which you are blessing someone, your good intentions may sometimes stumble in trying to find the right words of comfort. It is easy to offend without meaning to by offering what sound like platitudes to those who are in the immediate throes of suffering. It is also easy to give impressions of God that hurt rather than help them. The texts of these rites will assist you to reflect on how to focus your comments. They are also impersonal enough that they offer room for participants in the rites to take them as words from God to be pondered and applied to their own experience rather than as personal remarks about their own faith response to what they have suffered.

On a practical note, all of the orders recommend an opening and closing song. If they are celebrated in a public setting, with advanced preparation, music may be an effective option because it engages the human spirit so deeply and speaks so strongly at a level beyond words. However, if you are visiting alone, you may or may not be able to supply this element, and participants may or may not be able join in. Encourage liturgical musicians to join the minister of care. Find out if the place you are going to has music resources, or if you will need to bring worship aids, song books, or hymnals.

HOLY COMMUNION

This book provides two rites for lay ministers to give Holy Communion to the sick: "Communion in Ordinary Circumstances" and "Communion in a Hospital or Institution."

Communion in Ordinary Circumstances: The first form, called "Communion in Ordinary Circumstances," is especially useful if you are taking Holy Communion to the sick or aging in their homes. It assumes two things: First, that you have enough time to lead the full rite of Holy Communion including a short Liturgy of the Word; second, that those you visit are well enough to participate in a full service. The Church urges us always to consider the needs of the sick or aging. If they are very weak or tire quickly, it's better to shorten or omit elements like the explanation after the reading or the General Intercessions (Prayer of the Faithful), or simply to use the shorter form called "Communion in a Hospital or Institution" even in a home setting.

Communion in a Hospital or Institution: This second form, "Communion in a Hospital or Institution," provides a minimal format mainly intended for use when you are visiting many patients individually in an institutional setting. The Church expresses a strong preference for avoiding this abbreviated format even in an institution. Instead, it is suggested that, if possible, you gather several residents together in one or more areas and celebrate the full rite of "Communion in Ordinary Circumstances." If that is not possible, the Church recommends that you add elements from the fuller rite, such as the reading of the word, unless participants are too weak. On the other hand, in the case of extremely sick people, you may shorten "Communion in a Hospital or Institution" by omitting as much of the rite as necessary. Try to include at least a greeting, the Lord's Prayer, the customary responses that precede Holy Communion itself, and the closing prayer.

PASTORAL CARE OF THE DYING

Viaticum: Holy Communion for the Dying: Any of the seriously ill, but especially hospice patients, may move more quickly than expected toward death. A person who faces death within days should receive Holy Communion under the form of Viaticum. "Viaticum" means something like "travel with you," but it is often translated as food for the journey. Although the sacrament of Anointing of the Sick strengthens us in the face of sickness, Eucharist as Viaticum is the sacrament that, together with Penance, prepares a person for the final journey through death to everlasting life in Christ. Catholics are obligated to receive Viaticum if possible. The sacrament of Anointing of the Sick may be given after Penance but *before* Viaticum. If the person is unable to swallow, they may receive the Sacrament of Penance *instead* of Viaticum; however, the Church teaches that Viaticum is the essential sacrament when we are in the face of death. The time for using the special comforting and strengthening prayers of the Rite of Viaticum to administer Holy Communion is while the person is still conscious and able to swallow. Once death has become imminent, dying persons may receive Viaticum every day for as long as they are able. An Extraordinary Minister of Holy Communion may and should give Viaticum to the dying. If the dying person has not received sacramental absolution, please make sure the person has the opportunity for both the Sacrament of Penance and, if desired, Anointing of the Sick.

Commendation for the Dying and Prayers for the Dead: While the sacraments, especially Viaticum, unite the dying with Christ in his passage from this life to the next, we also gather with the dying and those around them to sustain this union through the prayer and faith of the Church.

"Commendation for the Dying" does not follow a fixed pattern. You may select any texts from the prayers, litanies, aspirations, psalms and readings, or you may use other familiar prayers, such as the rosary. If you have had the opportunity to talk with the dying person and loved ones or others present, choose texts you think will sustain and strengthen them according to their spiritual needs and other circumstances. Pray the texts slowly and quietly, allowing ample opportunities for silence. You may repeat them as often as needed, especially prayers that have special meaning for those present. Even the dying who are unconscious can sometimes hear more than we realize. If the dying cannot hear, loved ones present will find comfort in the prayers.

If you minister in an institutional setting, you may find that those who are not Catholic will ask you to pray with and for them. You may use these texts with and for any who are in need of the consolation of prayer. The texts drawn from the Bible are especially likely to bring comfort.

Once death has occurred, you will find both prayers for the dead and prayers for family and friends on page 134, "Prayers for the Dead."

Ritual Preparation: All of the rites are simple to follow. Look them over before making your visits in order to familiarize yourself with the order of prayer. Directions are included and parts are clearly marked so that you can easily lead the communicants in prayer. The texts of the rites included in this book are specifically for lay ministers.

THE GOSPEL FOR SUNDAYS AND HOLY DAYS OF OBLIGATION

Following the rites is the Gospel for Sundays and holy days of obligation for Year B. Remember the Church has a three year cycle of readings. In 2010 the readings will be from Year C. The Church recommends reading the week's Sunday Gospel during the Communion rite as one important way of uniting the communicants in spirit with the parish from which sickness or age has separated them.

In this book, the Gospel is clearly labeled by date and the title of particular observances so that you can easily find the appropriate reading. For example, if you make your visit during the Second Week of Ordinary Time, you will use the Gospel for the Second Sunday of Ordinary Time. In 2009, this Sunday of Ordinary Time is January 18. Simply look for the date and the title of the celebration and you will know which Gospel to use. These are also indicated in the table of contents of this book. For some observances, such as Palm Sunday, the Lectionary provides a longer and shorter form of the Gospel. For simplicity, only the shorter form is included in this resource.

If you are visiting on a holy day of obligation, use the Gospel prescribed for these days. You can also locate the Gospel for holy days of obligation by date and title. In the dioceses of the United States of America, the holy days of obligation occurring in 2009, liturgical year B, are:

- Solemnity of the Immaculate Conception of the Blessed Virgin Mary (December 8, 2008)

- Solemnity of the Nativity of the Lord (December 25, 2008)

- Solemnity of the Blessed Virgin Mary, the Mother of God (January 1, 2009)

- Solemnity of the Ascension of the Lord (May 21 or May 24, 2009)

- Solemnity of All Saints (November 1, 2009)

"Regarding the Ascension of the Lord, the ecclesiastical Provinces [dioceses] of Boston, Hartford, New York, Newark, Philadelphia, and the state of Nebraska have retained its proper celebration on the proper Thursday [May 21, 2009]. In these Provinces [dioceses], the readings for the day are from the solemnity of the Ascension of the Lord. In all other Provinces [dioceses] that have transferred this solemnity to the Seventh Sunday of Easter, on that day (7th Sunday of Easter), the readings are from the Ascension of the Lord" (www.usccb.org/norms/1246.htm).

Please also note that the solemnity of the Assumption of the Blessed Virgin Mary (August 15) is *not* a holy day of obligation in 2009 because it falls on a Saturday.

If you are visiting very young sick children, you might want to obtain a copy of the appropriate reading from the *Lectionary for Masses with Children* from your parish. Another option is to read the Gospel recommended in "Visits to a Sick Child."

If you are praying with those who are struggling with addictions, the aftermath of violence, or with parents who have suffered the loss of a child through miscarriage, you will usually find the readings recommended in the orders of blessing more appropriate to their circumstances than the Gospel for the Sunday. However, if appropriate, feel free to use the Gospel for Sundays and holy days of obligation. To discern which readings to use, it is best to look over the order of service *before* the visit occurs.

EXPLANATION OF THE READINGS

You will notice that the rites offer an opportunity for the Minister of Care to give a brief explanation of the reading with special reference to the experience of those with whom you are praying and, where appropriate, of their caregivers. If you are using the Sunday or holy day reading, you might want to base your explanation and reflection on the parish Sunday homily in order to deepen the sense of connection you are trying encourage. If you feel uncomfortable about speaking, you will find a brief explanation of the reading after the Gospel for each Sunday and holy day. If you choose to read it from the book, it would be a good idea to ponder it and make it your own so that the words come from your heart and not merely from the page. The Word of God itself creates a bond between reader and hearers, breaking down the sense of isolation that afflicts sufferers. Explanatory words that are spoken, or even read, with sincerity and personal conviction will support this pastoral relationship more effectively than words read mechanically.

PATRON SAINTS

Finally, there is a list of saints who the Church has identified as particular intercessors, companions, and guides for those suffering various kinds of afflictions, whether physical or emotional. If you feel that those with whom you pray would welcome the company and support of a saint, you might want to include the saint's name in the intercessions (petitions) and suggest that those you are visiting continue to ask for the saint's help. An example of an intercession is:

For all those who suffer from throat cancer,
   especially N. (insert the name of the person or
   persons present), that through the intercession
   of Saint Blaise, may find comfort and strength,
   we pray to the Lord.

This book does not provide any information about the saints listed, but there are many books and Web sites where you can find their stories. Such resources are *Butler's Lives of the Saints* (published by the Liturgical Press), Catholic Online, (www.catholic.org/saints), and the Catholic Forum (www. catholic-forum.com/saints/).

BEYOND THE BOOK

The official rites offer appropriate prayers and clear directions, but they don't tell you everything you need to know in order to lead the rituals effectively. Here are some practical hints that may help.

GETTING FROM THE PARISH CHURCH TO YOUR PASTORAL ASSIGNMENT

Scheduling a Visit: Some parishes assign ministers to visit particular people but encourage them to make their own arrangements regarding the day and time. Both those in need of your ministry and their families or caregivers, at home or in institutional facilities, appreciate being able to negotiate appropriate times for a pastoral visit or Holy Communion. It gives them an opportunity to make sure that they and those they would like to have present can be there. For example, if you're visiting the sick, you don't want to drop in when patients are absent from their rooms for tests or treatments.

If you are asked to take Holy Communion to the sick and the homebound at times other than during Sunday Mass, please make sure your training includes information about where to find the tabernacle key and how to approach the tabernacle reverently, open it, and transfer the hosts you will need from the ciborium in which they are kept to the container you will use to carry the Blessed Sacrament to the sick (see below). It is particularly important to arrange with the parish coordinator a convenient time for you to obtain the tabernacle key, because it is not permitted to keep the Eucharist at home or carry it all day as you go about your ordinary business before visiting communicants.

Ordinarily, when taking the Blessed Sacrament from the tabernacle, you would pray briefly before the tabernacle, wash your fingers in a small vessel of water that is usually kept beside the tabernacle for that purpose, wipe them on a finger towel also usually kept there, and genuflect after opening the tabernacle. If your parish does not provide either the small vessel or finger towel, wash your hands in the sacristy or otherwise clean your fingers as best you are able over the sacrarium (a sink flowing directly into the ground for water from purifications, from the first washings of the altar cloths, or the water containing the completely dissolved consecrated hosts which cannot be properly consumed).

If you have unused hosts left over at the end of your rounds, you must bring them back to the parish church and replace them in the tabernacle. After closing the tabernacle, you again wash your fingers. You may also cleanse the empty pyx (a dignified vessel, often round, used to carry the consecrated host) in the sacrarium if it appears to contain crumbs. Fill it with water, drink the water, and dry the pyx carefully on a finger towel, if available.

If you wish to avoid having hosts that must be returned, you can give the last few communicants more than one host so that all the hosts are consumed or consume them yourself as part of the communion rite during your last visit, provided all the usual requirements for communion are met. However, you may not simply consume them yourself after your last visit because Holy Communion is always received in the context of public prayer rather than simply as a matter of convenience by the minister alone. Similarly, you may not take the remaining hosts home to return later to the Church because the Eucharist must be kept in a tabernacle or other designated locked place of reservation in a church.

Bringing What You Need: Make a checklist of what you want to have with you before you leave home. You'll find some suggestions below. Don't forget this book! It does happen. If it does, don't panic, and don't fail to keep your appointment. As a precaution, make every effort to memorize the outline of the rites you expect to use or keep a copy of a simple outline in your pocket, wallet, or purse. In this case, do make up your own prayer, but keep it very short and simple. Borrow a Bible or summarize the Gospel in your own words. God works through all our weaknesses and mistakes.

Carrying the Blessed Sacrament: The Blessed Sacrament is in the pyx or in another dignified vessel reserved exclusively for that purpose. Your parish will probably supply you with what you need. Some pyxes can be worn or carried in a pouch on a cord around the neck. When you are carrying the Blessed Sacrament, remember and attend reverently to Christ, choosing your activities appropriately, without becoming artificially silent or stilted in your conversation, especially with those who are not aware of what you are carrying or of its significance. On the one hand, avoid distractions such as loud music, "talk" programs or other television shows, movies or DVDs/tapes, or other things that would disturb prayer while you are en route. On the other hand, while avoiding such distractions, be careful not to be rude to people who greet you or speak to you in passing as you walk to your destination. Christ is not offended by the company and conversation of human beings! You should make your Communion visit immediately upon leaving the Church.

Music Preparation: Music most certainly can be included in the rites and orders of blessing. Singing familiar melodies and texts can be extremely comforting and healing to those who are suffering. Hospitals, nursing homes, and other facilities might have a piano or you might bring a guitar. A capella singing can be just as effective. Be sure to select music in which either the refrain is simple or are familiar melodies, and that the texts give a message of Christ's hope. Here are some suggestions: *Blest Are They; Jesus, Heal Us; Healer of Our Every Ill; Lord of All Hopefulness; I Heard the Voice of Jesus Say; Remember Your Love; Shepherd Me, O God; You Are Mine.*

PREPARING AN ENVIRONMENT FOR PRAYER

ENCOUNTERING CHRIST IN PERSONS

Church ministry is always personal. It is important that you spend a few minutes at the beginning of your visit to get to know those present and give them a chance to feel comfortable with you. Your parish may be able to supply you with helpful information in advance of your visit. In return, it would be useful to other Ministers of Care if you were to report back what you had learned about the condition, circumstances, and needs of those you visit.

When you arrive, put those present at ease by engaging in a few moments of personal conversation. Tell them your name and remind them that the parish has sent you. Ask how they are and listen attentively to their answers. If you are visiting the sick, show your interest and concern, but remember that you are not there to offer medical advice or to pass judgment on medical matters, even if you yourself are a professional medical caregiver. If you can, address those you are visiting by name, but be aware that not everyone likes to be addressed by a first name without permission. Sickness, debilitating aging, and other forms of public suffering often rob people of their sense of personal dignity, so treating people with respect is an important dimension of your ministry. Whatever their condition, you and they are both collaborators in Christ's work. Ministry is a two-way street: those whom you visit are serving you by their witness to Christ suffering as much as you are serving them by offering them Christ's loving comfort. Take note of any special needs you see: is the sufferer low on energy, in pain, limited in motion, hard of hearing, angry, sad, or seemingly depressed? You will want to tailor the length, content, and style of the celebration accordingly.

PREPARING YOURSELF TO LEAD PRAYER

The world of the suffering, especially those confined to home or, even more so, to a hospital or geriatric facility may not feel much like a place of prayer. The most important element in creating an environment for prayer is you. The minister who prays while leading others in prayer is the most powerful invitation one can offer to those who need to be called from all the preoccupations of suffering into deeper awareness of the mystery of God present and acting in our midst.

Here are some steps you can take to develop this important skill:

1) Devote time for praying, reading, and meditating on the texts of the prayers and readings provided in this book. You will best pray them in public if you have already prayed them many times in private.

2) Familiarize yourself thoroughly with the structure and flow of the rites so that you can concentrate on the people rather than the book. You need not memorize prayers or readings. Simply know what comes next and where to find it.

3) Before you go into the building or room, pray briefly, asking Christ to work through you; after the visit, pause to give thanks.

4) Reflect on your experience after you return home. Were there moments during the celebration when you felt uncertain or distracted? Why? What could you do next time to make yourself more at ease so that you can pray more attentively without losing contact with those you are leading in prayer? Sharing experience with other Ministers of Care or parish staff can be a useful way to continue and deepen everyone's continuing ministry formation.

PREPARING THE ROOM FOR PRAYER

You can also take some simple steps to establish an atmosphere that encourages prayer when circumstances allow. A small standing crucifix, cross, or icon heightens consciousness of Christ. Appropriate lighting can help, where possible. In an institutional setting, for example, a lamp or sunlight creates a more humane environment than do fluorescent lights. If you are taking Holy Communion to someone, take a small white cloth and a candle with you to prepare a place on which to put the pyx containing the Blessed Sacrament as a focus for the celebration as you lead the other prayers. (Be sure you have something with which to light the candle!) A corporal (traditionally a square white, linen cloth upon which is placed sacred vessels holding the Blessed Sacrament) is not required, but if it is used, it is traditionally placed on top of another white cloth rather than on a bare surface. Caregivers familiar with the rite may have prepared a place in advance, but many will not.

Be aware of the restrictions you may face in a health care or geriatric facility. The Communion rite recommends that the minister be accompanied by a candle-bearer and place a candle on the table where the Blessed Sacrament will stand during the celebration, as described above. However, safety regulations usually forbid the use of open flames in institutions. Oxygen and other substances that might be in use are highly flammable. Moreover, you may not be able to find any appropriate surface other than a bedside table or night stand that will have to be cleared before you can set up a place for the Blessed Sacrament. Be prepared to make whatever practical adjustments the circumstances require. If you have never visited a particular hospital unit or nursing home, see if you can find another minister who has and find out what to expect.

PREPARING PARTICIPANTS FOR PRAYER

After a few moments of conversation, find a graceful way to end the social part of the visit without seeming uninterested or abrupt. Then give the participants a simple, brief overview of the rite you will be using so they will know what to expect, unless you know they are already familiar with the rite. Surprises tend to disrupt prayer! It's especially important to decide in advance who will do the reading. The directions say that the reading may be done "by one of those present or by the minister." If you don't know the participants, the best solution might be to ask for a volunteer (and allow the volunteer a few moments to prepare), but remember that not everyone is willing or able to read in public with short notice, especially in times of distress. Finally, mark the beginning of prayer clearly by inviting silent attentiveness, making the sign of the cross and moving into the service itself.

RECOGNIZING THE RECIPIENT

You are ministering not only to those to whom the ritual is addressed but also to those around them, whether loved ones or caregivers. Be sure to include them by looking and speaking to them, as well as to the person who is your focus. When you are saying prayers of blessing over the sufferer, your attention is on that person alone, but all present are invited to join in the "Amen" that affirms and concludes the prayer. Practice with another minister until you can say prayers in such a way that others know when and how to respond without having a book in front of them.

WHO MAY RECEIVE HOLY COMMUNION

Catholic shut-ins, caregivers, or others who assemble with them may receive Holy Communion provided the usual conditions have been met. You can offer that invitation before you begin the Communion rite, being careful not to embarrass or offend those who are not eligible to receive. "The elderly, the infirm and those who care for them can receive the Holy Eucharist even if they have eaten something within the preceding hour" (Code of Canon Law,919 §2).

Special Circumstances

Unfortunately, neither sickness nor the deterioration sometimes brought on by aging is neat or predictable. The physical, psychological, and spiritual condition of those you visit may have changed since the arrangements for your visit were made. You may need to make unprepared changes in the rite or blessing you are using to meet the current need.

Extraordinary Ministers of Holy Communion: If you are taking Holy Communion to the sick or elderly, sometimes those you are visiting will express reluctance to receive. They may or may not want to tell you why. They might be embarrassed to say that they are too nauseated; they might feel alienated from God; they might need sacramental absolution but don't want to say so. You are obviously a person of generosity and compassion, or you wouldn't have volunteered to be an Extraordinary Minister of Holy Communion. However, a Holy Communion visit is not ordinarily the best time to identify and try to resolve serious personal or spiritual problems. Be aware of your status and of the vulnerability of the suffering: you represent the Church, and you have more power than you may realize to make others feel guilty by showing that you disapprove of their decision not to receive Holy Communion or by giving the impression that they have wasted your time. Remember that they are not rejecting you as a person. Rather, they are struggling with something deeper. Offer to pray with them, using the rites provided for visiting or blessing the sick. Invite them to enter more deeply into communion with the suffering and risen Christ who loves them. Let them know what pastoral resources are available to them: offer to return or to send another minister at a more convenient time; provide the parish phone number; offer to let the pastoral staff know that they would like a priest to visit, without forcing them to reply. If the parish distributes a bulletin during the weekend Masses, bring one along to leave with the person to whom you are visiting.

Sometimes you may find that those you are visiting are unable to swallow easily. Consult medical caregivers. If they give permission, you may break the host into the smallest of pieces, place a piece on the person's tongue to dissolve, and follow with a glass of water to make swallowing possible. Be careful with crumbs when you break the host. The best thing to do is to break the host carefully over the pyx so that crumbs will fall into the pyx. If any crumbs fall on the cloth or table on which the pyx has been placed, moisten your finger, pick up all the crumbs very carefully, and consume them reverently.

You may even find that someone cannot ingest the host at all. In such cases, the person may receive the Blood of Christ, but that requires specialized vessels and procedures. Report the circumstances to your pastor, parish coordinator, or to the facility chaplain's office if the person is in a health care or geriatric facility. They will be able to appropriately give Holy Communion. In the meantime, use one of the rites for visiting or blessing the sick to give them the support of your presence and prayer.

Be aware that the hospitalized may not be permitted to take anything by mouth for a period of time prior to certain tests or treatments. Even a small piece of the host received at such times may cause medical personnel to cancel the planned procedure. If you see a sign that says "Nothing by mouth" or "NPO," initials for the Latin phrase (*nil per os*) meaning the same thing, ask a member of the medical staff if you may administer Holy Communion, but expect a "no." In this case, too, you should still pray with the sick or aging, using one of the rites for visiting or blessing the sick. Remember that you still offer them the comfort of Christ's presence in his word and through your own presence and that of the parish you represent.

Don't be alarmed by moments of silence. Sometimes ministers think they need to fill silences with conversation or action. There is nothing wrong with sitting in silence with another. In fact, these can be quite healing moments. God is present in these moments.

You should also be cognizant of those who are either not able to speak, have difficulty speaking, or speak rather slowly. Be patient and allow them to respond as they are able.

It is important that the Extraordinary Minister of Holy Communion keeps in mind the sacramental rites which are an essential part of the Church's ministry to the sick and dying and which can be administered *only* by an ordained bishop or priest—the sacraments of Penance (Reconciliation) and the Anointing of the Sick. As appropriate, it is part of your ministry to bring these to the attention of the sick and those confined to their homes, and if needed, to help them contact a priest.

SERVICE TO THE PEOPLE OF GOD

Among these nuts and bolts of the ministry of care, never lose sight of your purpose. You have been commissioned in the name of Christ and his Church to serve as a bridge builder across the isolation that separates the sick and suffering from the parish community of faith and worship. Your deepest task is to carry the good news of the Gospel to those who stand in need of its healing power. With your parish or diocesan training program, the support of your parish pastoral staff and other Ministers of Care, this book and your growing experience, you have many of the tools you will need. However, the most important tool is one that only Christ can provide for you. The more deeply you yourself enter into the heart of the Gospel message, the more clearly you will see that sick and healthy, young and old, grieving and rejoicing, struggling and at peace, are all one Body. In that Body, we are *all* servants of the Good news we proclaim, building one another up in faith and love until that day when, by God's gracious gift, we will all dwell together in the Lord's own house for ever and ever.

Genevieve Glen, OSB
Abbey of Saint Walburga
Virginia Dale, CO
Revised January 2007

Author Information:
Sister Genevieve Glen, OSB, is a Benedictine nun of the contemplative Abbey of St. Walburga in Virginia Dale, CO. She holds master's degrees in systematic theology from Saint John's University, Collegeville, MN, and in spirituality from the Catholic University of America in Washington DC, where she also did extensive doctoral studies in liturgy. She has lectured and written extensively on the Church's rites for the sick and dying. She is co-author of the *Handbook for Ministers of Care*, second edition (Liturgy Training Publications) and contributing editor of *Recovering the Riches of Anointing: A Study of the Sacrament of the Sick* (The Liturgical Press).

THE RITES

Orders for the Blessing of the Sick

INTRODUCTION

376   The blessing of the sick by the ministers of the Church is a very ancient custom, having its origins in the practice of Christ himself and his apostles. When ministers visit those who are sick, they are to respect the provisions of *Pastoral Care of the Sick: Rites of Anointing and Viaticum*, nos. 42–56, but the primary concern of every minister should be to show the sick how much Christ and his Church are concerned for them.

377   The text of *Pastoral Care of the Sick* indicates many occasions for blessing the sick and provides the blessing for formularies.[13]

378   The present order may be used by a priest or deacon. It may also be used by a layperson, who follows the rites and prayers designated for a lay minister. While maintaining the structure and chief elements of the rite, the minister should adapt the celebration to the circumstances of the place and the people involved.

379   When just one sick person is to be blessed, a priest or deacon may use the short formulary given in no. 406.

---

13.   See Roman Ritual, *Pastoral Care of the Sick: Rites of Anointing and Viaticum*, no. 54.

ORDER OF BLESSING

A. ORDER FOR THE BLESSING OF ADULTS
INTRODUCTORY RITES

380   *When the community has gathered, the minister says:*

In the name of the Father, and of the Son, and of the Holy Spirit.

All make the sign of the cross and reply:

Amen.

382   *A lay minister greets those present in the following words.*

Brothers and sisters, let us bless the Lord, who went about doing good and healing the sick. Blessed be God now and for ever.
R. *Blessed be God now and for ever.*

Or:

R. *Amen.*

383   *In the following or similar words, the minister prepares the sick and all present for the blessing.*

The Lord Jesus, who went about doing good works and healing sickness and infirmity of every kind, commanded his disciples to care for the sick, to pray for them, and to lay hands on them. In this celebration we shall entrust our sick brothers and sisters to the care of the Lord, asking that he will enable them to bear their pain and suffering in the knowledge that, if they accept their share in the pain of his own passion, they will also share in its power to give comfort and strength.

READING OF THE WORD OF GOD

384   A reader, another person present, or the minister reads a text of sacred Scripture, taken preferably from the texts given in Pastoral Care of the Sick *and the* Lectionary for Mass.[14] *The readings chosen should be those that best apply to the physical and spiritual condition of those who are sick.*

Brothers and Sisters, listen to the words of the second letter of Paul to the Corinthians: 1:3–7

The God of all consolation.

Blessed be the God and Father of our Lord Jesus Christ, the Father of compassion and God of all encouragement, who encourages us in our every affliction, so that we may be able to encourage those who are in any affliction with the encouragement with which we ourselves are encouraged by God. For as Christ's sufferings overflow to us, so through Christ does our encouragement also overflow. If we are afflicted, it is for your encouragement and salvation; if we are encouraged, it is for your encouragement, which enables you to endure the same sufferings that we suffer. Our hope for you is firm, for we know that as you share in the sufferings, you also share in the encouragement.

---

14. See ibid, no. 297; Lectionary for Mass (2nd ed., 1981), nos. 790–795, 796–800 (Ritual Masses: V. Pastoral Care of the Sick and the Dying, 1. Anointing of the Sick and 2. Viaticum), and nos. 933–937 (Masses for Various Needs and Occasions, III. For Various Public Needs, 24. For the Sick).

385   Or:

**Brothers and sisters, listen to the words of the
holy gospel according to Matthew:**   11:28–30

Come to me and I will refresh you.

Jesus said to the crowds: "Come to me, all you who
labor and are burdened, and I will give you rest. Take
my yoke upon you and learn from me, for I am meek
and humble of heart; and you will find rest for yourselves. For my yoke is easy, and my burden light."

386   Or:

**Brothers and sisters, listen to the words of the holy
gospel according to Mark:**   6:53–56

They laid the sick in the marketplace

After making the crossing, Jesus and his disciples
came to land at Gennesaret and tied up there. As
they were leaving the boat, people immediately
recognized him. They scurried about the surrounding
country and began to bring in the sick on mats to
wherever they heard he was. Whatever villages or
towns or countryside he entered, they laid the sick in
the marketplaces and begged him that they might
touch only the tassel on his cloak; and as many as
touched it were healed.

387   *As circumstances suggest, one of the following responsorial psalms may
be sung or said, or some other suitable song.*

R. *Lord, you have preserved my life from destruction.*

Isaiah 38

Once I said,
"In the noontime of life I must depart!
To the gates of the nether world I shall
be consigned
for the rest of my years." **R.**

I said, "I shall see the LORD no more
in the land of the living.
No longer shall I behold my fellow men
among those who dwell in the world." **R.**

My dwelling, like a shepherd's tent,
is struck down and borne away from me;
You have folded up my life, like a weaver
who severs the last thread. **R.**

Those live whom the LORD protects;
yours . . . the life of my spirit.
You have given me health and life. **R.**

Psalm 102:2–3, 24–25

R. *(v. 2) O Lord, hear my prayer, and let my cry come
to you.*

388   *As circumstances suggest, the minister may give those present a brief
explanation of the biblical text, so that they may understand through faith the
meaning of the celebration.*

INTERCESSIONS

389   *The intercessions are then said. The minister introduces them and an*
assisting minister or one of those present announces the intentions. From the
following intentions those best suited to the occasion may be used or adapted,
or other intentions that apply to those who are sick and to the particular
circumstances may be composed.

The minister says:

The Lord Jesus loves our brothers and sisters who
are ill. With trust let us pray to him that he will
comfort them with his grace, saying:
R. *Lord, give those who are sick the comfort of*
your presence.

Assisting minister:

Lord Jesus, you came as healer of body and of spirit,
in order to cure all our ills. *R.*

Assisting minister:

You were a man of suffering, but it was our infirmities
that you bore, our sufferings that you endured. *R.*

Assisting minister:

You chose to be like us in all things, in order to
assure us of your compassion. *R.*

Assisting minister:

You experienced the weakness of the flesh in order to
deliver us from evil. *R.*

Assisting minister:

At the foot of the cross your Mother stood as
companion in your sufferings, and in your tender
care you gave her to us as our Mother. *R.*

Assisting minister:

It is your wish that in our own flesh we should fill up what is wanting in your sufferings for the sake of your Body, the Church. *R.*

390   *Instead of the intercessions or in addition to them, one of the following litanies taken from* Pastoral Care of the Sick, *nos. 245 and 138 may be used.*

Minister:

You bore our weakness and carried our sorrows: Lord, have mercy.

R. Lord, have mercy.

Minister:

You felt compassion for the crowd, and went about doing good and healing the sick: Christ, have mercy.

R. Christ, have mercy.

Minister:

You commanded your apostles to lay their hands on the sick in your name: Lord, have mercy.

R. Lord, have mercy.

391   *Or:*

The minister says:

Let us pray to God for our brothers and sisters and for all those who devote themselves to caring for them.

Assisting minister:

Bless *N.* and *N.* and fill them with new hope and strength: Lord, have mercy.

R. Lord, have mercy.

Relieve their pain: Lord, have mercy. **R.**

Assisting minister:

Free them from sin and do not let them give way to temptation: Lord, have mercy. **R.**

Assisting minister:

Sustain all the sick with your power: Lord, have mercy. **R.**

Assisting minister:

Assist all who care for the sick: Lord, have mercy. **R.**

Assisting minister:

Give life and health to our brothers and sisters on whom we lay our hands in your name: Lord, have mercy. **R.**

PRAYER OF BLESSING

394   *A lay minister traces the sign of the cross on the forehead of each sick person and says the following prayer of blessing.*

Lord, our God,
who watch over your creatures with unfailing care,
keep us in the safe embrace of your love.
With your strong right hand raise up your servants
     (*N.* and *N.*)
and give them the strength of your own power.

Minister to them and heal their illnesses,
so that they may have from you the help they
long for.

We ask this through Christ our Lord.
R. Amen.

395   *Or, for one sick person:*
Lord and Father, almighty and eternal God,
by your blessing you give us strength and support
in our frailty:
turn with kindness toward this your servant **N.**
Free him/her from all illness and restore him/her
to health,
so that in the sure knowledge of your goodness
he/she will gratefully bless your holy name.

We ask this through Christ our Lord.
R. Amen.

396   *After the prayer of blessing the minister invites all present to pray
for the protection of the Blessed Virgin. They may do so by singing or reciting
a Marian antiphon, for example,* We turn to you for protection (Sub tuum
praesidium) *or* Hail, Holy Queen.

CONCLUDING RITE

398   *A lay minister invokes the Lord's blessing on the sick and all present by
signing himself or herself with the sign of the cross and saying:*
May the Lord Jesus Christ,
who went about doing good and healing the sick,

grant that we may have good health
and be enriched by his blessings.
R. Amen.

B. ORDER FOR THE BLESSING OF CHILDREN

399   For the blessing of sick children, the texts already given are to be adapted
to the children's level, but special intercessions are provided here and a special
prayer of blessing.

INTERCESSIONS

400   To the following intentions others may be added that apply to the
condition of the sick children and to the particular circumstances.

The minister says:

The Lord Jesus loved and cherished the little ones
with a special love. Let us, then, pray to him for these
sick children, saying:
R. *Lord, keep them in all their ways.*

Or:

R. *Lord, hear our prayer.*

Assisting minister:

Lord Jesus, you called the little children to come to
you and said that the kingdom of heaven belongs to
such as these; listen with mercy to our prayers for
these children. (For this we pray:) *R.*

Assisting minister:

You revealed the mysteries of the kingdom of heaven,
not to the wise of this world, but to little children;

give these children the proof of your love. (For this
we pray:) **R.**

Assisting minister:

You praised the children who cried out their
Hosannas on the eve of your passion; strengthen
these children and their parents with your holy
comfort. (For this we pray:) **R.**

Assisting minister:

You charged your disciples to take care of the sick;
stand at the side of all those who so gladly devote
themselves to restoring the health of these children.
(For this we pray:) **R.**

PRAYER OF BLESSING

402   *A lay minister, and particularly a mother or father when blessing a sick
child, traces the sign of the cross on each child's forehead and then says the
following prayer of blessing.*

Father of mercy and God of all consolation,
you show tender care for all your creatures
and give health of soul and body.
Raise up these children
        (*or* this child *or* the son/daughter you have
            given us)
        from their (his/her) sickness.
Then, growing in wisdom and grace in your sight
        and ours,
they (he/she) will serve you all the days of their
        (his/her) life

in uprightness and holiness
and offer the thanksgiving due to your mercy.

We ask this through Christ our Lord.
R. Amen.

C. SHORTER RITE

403   *The minister says:*
Our help is in the name of the Lord.

All reply:
Who made heaven and earth.

404   *One of those present or the minister reads a text of sacred Scripture, for example:*

2 Corinthians 1:3–4
Blessed be the God and Father of our Lord Jesus
Christ, the Father of compassion and God of all
encouragement, who encourages us in our every
affliction, so that we may be able to encourage those
who are in any affliction with the encouragement
with which we ourselves are encouraged by God.

Matthew 11:28–29
Jesus said, "Come to me, all you who labor and
are burdened, and I will give you rest. Take my
yoke upon you and learn from me, for I am meek
and humble of heart; and you will find rest for
yourselves."

As circumstances suggest . . . a lay minister may trace the sign of the cross on the sick person's forehead while saying the prayer.

Lord and Father, almighty and eternal God,
by your blessing you give us strength and support in
  our frailty:
turn with kindness toward your servant, N.
Free him/her from all illness and restore him/her
  to health,
so that in the sure knowledge of your goodness
he/she will gratefully bless your holy name.

We ask this through Christ our Lord.
R. Amen.

Order for the Blessing of a Person Suffering from Addiction or from Substance Abuse

INTRODUCTION

407   Addiction to alcohol, drugs, and other controlled substances causes great disruption in the life of an individual and his or her family. This blessing is intended to strengthen the addicted person in the struggle to overcome addiction and also to assist his or her family and friends.

408   This blessing may also be used for individuals who, although not addicted, abuse alcohol or drugs and wish the assistance of God's blessing in their struggle.

409   Ministers should be aware of the spiritual needs of a person suffering from addiction or substance abuse, and to this end the pastoral guidance on the care of the sick and rites of *Pastoral Care of the Sick* will be helpful.

410   If the recovery process is slow or is marked by relapses, the blessing may be repeated when pastorally appropriate.

411   These orders may be used by a priest or a deacon, and also by a lay person, who follows the rites and prayers designated for a lay minister.

A. ORDER OF BLESSING

INTRODUCTORY RITES

412   *When the community has gathered, a suitable song may be sung. After the singing the minister says:*

In the name of the Father, and of the Son, and of the Holy Spirit.

All make the sign of the cross and reply:

Amen.

414   *A lay minister greets those present in the following words:*

Let us praise God our creator, who gives us courage and strength, now and for ever.

R. Amen.

415   *In the following or similar words, the minister prepares those present for the blessing.*

God created the world and all things in it and entrusted them into our hands that we might use them for our good and for the building up of the Church and human society. Today we pray for N., that God may strengthen him/her in his/her weakness and restore him/her to the freedom of God's children. We pray also for ourselves that we may encourage and support him/her in the days ahead.

READING OF THE WORD OF GOD

416   *A reader, another person present, or the minister reads a text of sacred Scripture.*

Brothers and sisters, listen to the words of the second letter of Paul to the Corinthians: 4:6–9

We are afflicted, but not crushed.

For God who said, "Let light shine out of darkness," has shone in our hearts to bring to light the knowledge of the glory of God on the face of Jesus Christ.

But we hold this treasure in earthen vessels, that the surpassing power may be of God and not from us. We are afflicted in every way, but not constrained; perplexed, but not driven to despair; persecuted, but not abandoned; struck down, but not destroyed.

417   *Or:*

Isaiah 63:7–9—He has favored us according to his mercy.

Romans 8:18–25—I consider the sufferings of the present to be as nothing compared with the glory to be revealed in us.

Matthew 15:21–28—Woman, you have great faith.

418   *As circumstances suggest, one of the following responsorial psalms may be sung or said, or some other suitable song.*

R. *Our help is from the Lord who made heaven and earth.*

Psalm 121

I lift up my eyes toward the mountains;
whence shall help come to me?

My help is from the LORD
who made heaven and earth. **R.**

May he not suffer your foot to slip;
may he slumber not who guards you:
Indeed he neither slumbers nor sleeps,
the guardian of Israel. **R.**

The LORD is your guardian; the LORD is your shade;
he is beside you at your right hand.
The sun shall not harm you by day,
nor the moon by night. **R.**

The LORD will guard you from all evil;
he will guard your life.
The LORD will guard your coming and your going,
both now and forever. **R.**

Psalm 130:1–2, 3–4, 5–6, 7–8
R. (v. 5) My soul trusts in the Lord.

419   As circumstances suggest, the minister may give those present a brief
explanation of the biblical text, so that they may understand through faith the
meaning of the celebration.

INTERCESSIONS

420   The intercessions are then said. The minister introduces them and an
assisting minister or one of those present announces the intentions. From the
following those best suited to the occasion may be used or adapted, or other
intentions that apply to the particular circumstances may be composed.

The minister says:

Our God gives us life and constantly calls us to new life; let us pray to God with confidence.

R. *Lord, hear our prayer.*

Assisting minister:

For those addicted to alcohol/drugs, that God may be their strength and support, we pray. **R.**

Assisting minister:

For **N.**, bound by the chains of addiction/substance abuse, that we encourage and assist him/her in his/her struggle, we pray. **R.**

Assisting minister:

For **N.**, that he/she may trust in the mercy of God through whom all things are possible, we pray. **R.**

Assisting minister:

For the family and friends of **N.**, that with faith and patience they show him/her their love, we pray. **R.**

Assisting minister:

For the Church, that it may always be attentive to those in need, we pray. **R.**

421 *After the intercessions the minister, in the following or similar words, invites all present to sing or say the Lord's Prayer.*

Let us pray to our merciful God as Jesus taught us:

All:

Our Father . . .

PRAYER OF BLESSING

422   A lay minister says the prayer with hands joined.

A   *For addiction*

God of mercy,
we bless you in the name of your Son, Jesus Christ,
who ministered to all who came to him.
Give your strength to N., your servant,
bound by the chains of addiction.
Enfold him/her in your love
and restore him/her to the freedom of God's children.

Lord,
look with compassion on all those
who have lost their health and freedom.
Restore to them the assurance of your
        unfailing mercy,
and strengthen them in the work of recovery.

To those who care for them,
grant patient understanding and a love
        that perseveres.

We ask this through Christ our Lord.
R. Amen.

B   *For substance abuse*

God of mercy,
we bless you in the name of your Son, Jesus Christ,

who ministered to all who came to him.
Give your strength to N., your servant,
enfold him/her in your love
and restore him/her to the freedom of God's children.

Lord,
look with compassion on all those
who have lost their health and freedom.
Restore to them the assurance of your
        unfailing mercy,
strengthen them in the work of recovery,
and help them to resist all temptation.

To those who care for them,
grant patient understanding and a love
        that perseveres.

We ask this through Christ our Lord.
R. Amen.

As circumstances suggest, the minister in silence may sprinkle the person with
holy water.

CONCLUDING RITE

424   A lay minister concludes the rite by signing himself or herself with the sign of the cross and saying:

May our all-merciful God, Father, Son, and Holy Spirit, bless us and embrace us in love for ever.
R. Amen.

425   It is preferable to end the celebration with a suitable song.

B. SHORTER RITE

426   All make the sign of the cross as the minister says:

Our help is in the name of the Lord.

All reply:

Who made heaven and earth.

427   One of those present or the minister reads a text of sacred Scripture, for example:

Brothers and sisters, listen to the words of the second letter of Paul to the Corinthians: 4:6–9

We are afflicted, but not crushed.

For God who said, "Let light shine out of darkness," has shone in our hearts to bring to light the knowledge of the glory of God on the face of Jesus Christ.

But we hold this treasure in earthen vessels, that the surpassing power may be of God and not from us. We are afflicted in every way, but not constrained; perplexed, but not driven to despair; persecuted, but not abandoned; struck down, but not destroyed.

428   Or:

Isaiah 63:7–9—*He has favored us according to his mercy.*

Matthew 15:21–28—*Woman, you have great faith.*

429   *A lay minister says the prayer with hands joined.*

A   For addiction

God of mercy,
we bless you in the name of your Son, Jesus Christ,
who ministered to all who came to him.
Give your strength to N., your servant,
bound by the chains of addiction.
Enfold him/her in your love
and restore him/her to the freedom of God's children.

Lord,
look with compassion on all those
who have lost their health and freedom.
Restore to them the assurance of your
        unfailing mercy,
and strengthen them in the work of your recovery.

To those who care for them,
grant patient understanding and a love
        that perseveres.

We ask this through Christ our Lord.
R. Amen.

B *For substance abuse.*

God of mercy,
we bless you in the name of your Son, Jesus Christ,
who ministered to all who came to him.
Give your strength to N., your servant,
enfold him/her in your love
and restore him/her to the freedom of God's children.

Lord,
look with compassion on all those
who have lost their health and freedom.
Restore to them the assurance of your
        unfailing mercy,
strengthen them in the work of recovery,
and help them to resist all temptation.

To those who care for them,
grant patient understanding and a love
        that perseveres.

We ask this through Christ our Lord.
R. *Amen.*

Order for the Blessing of a Victim of Crime or Oppression

INTRODUCTION

430   The personal experience of a crime, political oppression, or social oppression can be traumatic and not easily forgotten. A victim often needs the assistance of others, and no less that of God, in dealing with this experience.

431   This blessing is intended to assist the victim and help him or her come to a state of tranquility and peace.

432   These orders may be used by a priest or a deacon, and also by a layperson, who follows the rites and prayers designated for a lay minister.

A. ORDER OF BLESSING

INTRODUCTORY RITES

433   *When the community has gathered, a suitable song may be sung. After the singing, the minister says:*

In the name of the Father, and of the Son, and of the Holy Spirit.

All make the sign of the cross and reply:

Amen.

435   *A lay minister greets those present in the following words:*

May the Lord grant us peace, now and for ever.
R. Amen.

436   *In the following or similar words, the minister prepares those present for the blessing.*

Throughout history God has manifested his love and care for those who have suffered from violence, hatred, and oppression. We commend N. to the healing mercy of God who binds up all our wounds and enfolds us in his gentle care.

READING OF THE WORD OF GOD

437   *A reader, another person present, or the minister reads a text of sacred Scripture.*

Brothers and sisters, listen to the words of the holy gospel according to Matthew: 10:28–33

Do not fear.

Jesus said to his disciples: "Do not be afraid of those who kill the body but cannot kill the soul; rather, be afraid of the one who can destroy both soul and body in Gehenna. Are not two sparrows sold for a small coin? Yet not one of them falls to the ground without your Father's knowledge. Even all the hairs of your head are counted. So do not be afraid; you are worth more than many sparrows. Everyone who acknowledges me before others I will acknowledge before my heavenly Father. But whoever denies me before others, I will deny before my heavenly Father."

438   *Or:*

Isaiah 59:6b–8, 15–18—The Lord is appalled by evil and injustice.

Job 3:1–26—Lamentation of Job.

Lamentations 3:1–24—I am one who knows affliction.

Lamentations 3:49–59—When I called, you came to my aid.

Micah 4:1–4—Every person shall sit undisturbed.

Matthew 5:1–10—The beatitudes.

Matthew 5:43–48—Love your enemies, pray for those who persecute you.

Luke 10:25–37—The good Samaritan.

439   *As circumstances suggest, one of the following responsorial psalms may be sung, or some other suitable song.*

R. The Lord is my strength and my salvation.

Psalm 140

Deliver me, O LORD, from evil men;
preserve me from violent men,
From those who devise evil in their hearts,
and stir up wars ever day. *R.*

Save me, O LORD, from the hands of the wicked;
preserve me from violent men
Who plan to trip up my feet—
the proud who have hidden a trap for me;
They have spread cords for a net;
by the wayside they have laid snares for me. *R.*

Grant not, O LORD, the desires of the wicked;
further not their plans.
Those who surround me lift up their heads;
may the mischief which they threaten
         overwhelm them. *R.*

I know that the LORD renders
justice to the afflicted, judgment to the poor.
Surely the just shall give thanks to your name;
the upright shall dwell in your presence. *R.*

Psalm 142:2–3, 4b–5, 6–7
R. (v. 6) You, O Lord, are my refuge.

Psalm 31:2–3a, 4–5, 15–16, 24–25
R. (v. 6) Into your hands I commend my spirit.

440   *As circumstances suggest, the minister may give those present a brief
explanation of the biblical text, so that they may understand through faith the
meaning of the celebration.*

INTERCESSIONS

441   *The intercessions are then said. The minister introduces them and an
assisting minister or one of those present announces the intentions. From the*

*following those best suited to the occasion may be used or adapted, or other
intentions that apply to the particular circumstances may be composed.*

The minister says:

Let us pray to the Lord God, the defender of the
weak and powerless, who delivered our ancestors
from harm.
R. *Deliver us from evil, O Lord.*

Assisting minister:

For N., that he/she may be freed from pain and fear,
we pray to the Lord. R.

Assisting minister:

For all who are victims of crime/oppression, we pray
to the Lord. R.

Assisting minister:

For an end to all acts of violence and hatred, we pray
to the Lord. R.

Assisting minister:

For those who harm others, that they may change
their lives and turn to God, we pray to the Lord. R.

442   *After the intercessions the minister, in the following or similar words,
invites all present to sing or say the Lord's Prayer.*

The Lord heals our wounds and strengthens us in
our weakness; let us pray as Christ has taught us:

All:

Our Father . . .

PRAYER OF BLESSING

443   A lay minister says the prayer with hands joined.

Lord God,
your own Son was delivered into the hands of
        the wicked,
yet he prayed for his persecutors
and overcame hatred with the blood of the cross.
Relieve the suffering of N.;
grant him/her peace of mind
and a renewed faith in your protection and care.

Protect us all from the violence of others,
keep us safe from the weapons of hate,
and restore to us tranquility and peace.

We ask this through Christ our Lord.
R. Amen.

As circumstances suggest, the minister in silence may sprinkle the person with holy water.

CONCLUDING RITE

445   A lay minister concludes the rite by signing himself or herself with the sing of the cross and saying:

May God bless us with his mercy,
strengthen us with his love,
and enable us to walk in charity and peace.
R. Amen.

446   It is preferable to end the celebration with a suitable song.

SHORTER RITE

447 *All make the sign of the cross as the minister says:*

Our help is in the name of the Lord.

All reply:

Who made heaven and earth.

448 *One of those present or the minister reads a text of sacred Scripture, for example:*

Brothers and sisters, listen to the words of the holy gospel according to Matthew: 10:28–33

Do not fear.

Jesus said to his disciples: "Do not be afraid of those who kill the body but cannot kill the soul; rather, be afraid of the one who can destroy both soul and body in Gehenna. Are not two sparrows sold for a small coin? Yet not one of them falls to the ground without your Father's knowledge. Even all the hairs of your head are counted. So do not be afraid; you are worth more than many sparrows. Everyone who acknowledges me before others I will acknowledge before my heavenly Father. But whoever denies me before others, I will deny before my heavenly Father."

449 *Or:*

Isaiah 59:6b–8, 15–18—The Lord is appalled by evil and injustice.

Job 3:1–26—Lamentation of Job.

Lamentations 3:1–24—I am a man who knows affliction.

Lamentations 3:49–59—When I called, you came to my aid.

Matthew 5:1–10—The beatitudes.

Luke 10:25–37—The good Samaritan.

450   A lay minister says the prayer with hands joined.

Lord God,
your own Son was delivered into the hands of
    the wicked
yet he prayed for his persecutors
and overcame hatred with the blood of the cross.
Relive the suffering of **N.**;
grant him/her peace of mind
and a renewed faith in your protection and care.

Protect us all from the violence of others,
keep us safe from the weapons of hate,
and restore to us tranquility and peace.

We ask this through Christ our Lord.
R. Amen.

Order for the Blessing of Parents after a Miscarriage

INTRODUCTION

279   In times of death and grief the Christian turns to the Lord for consolation and strength. This is especially true when a child dies before birth. This blessing is provided to assist the parents in their grief and console them with the blessing of God.

280   The minister should be attentive to the needs of the parents and other family members and to this end the introduction to the *Order of Christian Funerals*, Part II: Funeral Rites for Children will be helpful.

281   These orders may be used by a priest or deacon, and also by a layperson who follows the rites and prayers designated for a lay minister.

A. ORDER OF BLESSING

INTRODUCTORY RITES

282   When the community has gathered, a suitable song may be sung. The minister says:

In the name of the Father, and of the Son, and of the Holy Spirit.

All make the sign of the cross and reply:

Amen.

284   A lay minister greets those present in the following words:

Let us praise the Father of mercies, the God of all consolation. Blessed be God for ever.

R. *Blessed be God for ever.*

285   In the following or similar words, the minister prepares those present for the blessing.

For those who trust in God,
in the pain of sorrow there is consolation,
in the face of despair there is hope,
in the midst of death there is life.
N. and N., as we mourn the death of your child we place ourselves in the hands of God and ask for strength, for healing, and for love.

READING OF THE WORD OF GOD

286   A reader, another person present, or the minister reads a text of sacred Scripture.

Brothers and sisters, listen to the words of the book of Lamentations: 3:17–26

Hope in the Lord.

My soul is deprived of peace,
I have forgotten what happiness is;
I tell myself my future is lost,
all that I hoped for from the Lord.
The thought of my homeless poverty
is wormwood and gall;
Remembering it over and over
leaves my soul downcast within me.
But I will call this to mind,
as my reason to have hope:
The favors of the LORD are not exhausted,
his mercies are not spent;
They are renewed each morning,
so great is his faithfulness.
My portion is the LORD, says my soul;
therefore will I hope in him.
Good is the LORD to one who waits for him,
to the soul that seeks him;
It is good to hope in silence
for the saving help of the LORD.

287   *Or:*

Isaiah 49:8–13—In a time of favor I answer you, on the day of salvation I help you.

Romans 8:18–27—In hope we were saved.

Romans 8:26–31—If God is for us, who can be against us?

Colossians 1:9–12—We have been praying for you unceasingly.

Hebrews 5:7–10—Christ intercedes for us.

Luke 22:39–46—Agony in the garden.

288   As circumstances suggest, one of the following responsorial psalms may
be sung, or some other suitable song.

R. *To you, O Lord, I lift up my soul.*

Psalm 25

Your ways, O LORD, make known to me;
teach me your paths,
Guide me in your truth and teach me,
for you are God my savior,
and for you I wait all the day. **R.**

Remember that your compassion, O LORD,
and your kindness are from of old.
The sins of my youth and my frailties remember not;
in your kindness remember me
because of your goodness, O LORD. **R.**

Look toward me, and have pity on me,
for I am alone and afflicted.
Relieve the troubles of my heart,
and bring me out of my distress. **R.**

Preserve my life, and rescue me;
let me not be put to shame, for I take refuge in you.
Let integrity and uprightness preserve me,
because I wait for you, O LORD. **R.**

Psalm 143:1, 5–6, 8, 30
R. *(v. 1) O Lord, hear my prayer.*

289   *As circumstances suggest, the minister may give those present a brief explanation of the biblical text, so that they may understand through faith the meaning of the celebration.*

INTERCESSIONS

290   *The intercessions are then said. The minister introduces them and an assisting minister or one of those present announces the intentions. From the following those best suited to the occasion may be used or adapted, or other intentions that apply to the particular circumstances may be composed.*

The minister says:

Let us pray to God who throughout the ages has heard the cries of parents.
R. *Lord, hear our prayer.*

Assisting minister:

For N. and N., who know the pain of grief, that they may be comforted, we pray. R.

Assisting minister:

For this family, that it may find new hope in the midst of suffering, we pray. R.

Assisting minister:

For these parents, that they may learn from the example of Mary, who grieved by the cross of her Son, we pray. R.

Assisting minister:

For all who have suffered the loss of a child, that Christ may be their support, we pray. R.

291   *After the intercessions the minister, in the following or similar words, invites all present to sing or say the Lord's Prayer.*

Let us pray to the God of consolation and hope, as Christ has taught us:

All:

Our Father . . .

PRAYER OF BLESSING

292   *A minister who is a priest or deacon says the prayer of blessing with hands outstretched over the parents; a lay minister says the prayer with hands joined.*

Compassionate God,
soothe the hearts of N. and N.,
and grant that through the prayers of Mary,
who grieved by the cross of her Son,
you may enlighten their faith,
give hope to their hearts,
and peace to their lives.

Lord,
grant mercy to all the members of this family
and comfort them with the hope
that one day we will all live with you,
with your Son Jesus Christ, and the Holy Spirit,
for ever and ever.
R. Amen.

293   *Or:*

Lord,
God of all creation
we bless and thank you for your tender care.

Receive this life you created in love
and comfort your faithful people in their time of loss
with the assurance of your unfailing mercy.

We ask this through Christ our Lord.
R. Amen.

As circumstances suggest, the minister in silence may sprinkle the parents with holy water.

CONCLUDING RITE

295   *A lay minister concludes the rite by signing himself or herself with the sing of the cross and saying:*

May God give us peace in our sorrow,
consolation in our grief,
and strength to accept his will in all things.
R. Amen.

296   *It is preferable to end the celebration with a suitable song.*

SHORTER RITE

297   *All make the sign of the cross as the minister says:*
Our help is in the name of the Lord.

All reply:

Who made heaven and earth.

Brothers and sisters, listen to the words of the book
of Lamentations: 3:17–26

Hope in the Lord.

My soul is deprived of peace,
I have forgotten what happiness is;
I tell myself my future is lost,
all that I hoped for from the LORD.
The thought of my homeless poverty
is wormwood and gall;
Remembering it over and over
leaves my soul downcast within me.
But I will call this to mind,
as my reason to have hope:
The favors of the LORD are not exhausted,
his mercies are not spent;
They are renewed each morning,
so great is his faithfulness.
My portion is the LORD, says my soul;
therefore will I hope in him.
Good is the LORD to one who waits for him,
to the soul that seeks him;
It is good to hope in silence
for the saving help of the LORD.

299   *Or:*

Romans 8:26–31—If God is for us, who can be against us?

Colossians 1:9–12—We have been praying for you unceasingly.

300   *A lay minister says the prayer with hands joined.*

Compassionate God,
soothe the hearts of N. and N.,
and grant that through the prayers of Mary,
who grieved by the cross of her Son,
you may enlighten their faith,
give hope to their hearts,
and peace to their lives.

Lord,
grant mercy to all the members of this family
and comfort them with the hope
that one day we will all live with you,
with your Son Jesus Christ, and the Holy Spirit,
for ever and ever.
R. Amen.

301   *Or:*

Lord,
God of all creation,
we bless and thank you for your tender care.
Receive this life you created in love
and comfort your faithful people in their time of loss
with the assurance of your unfailing mercy.

We ask this through Christ our Lord.
R. Amen.

Pastoral Care of the Sick

INTRODUCTION

Lord, your friend is sick.

42   The rites in Part I of *Pastoral Care of the Sick: Rites of Anointing and Viaticum* are used by the Church to comfort the sick in time of anxiety, to encourage them to fight against illness, and perhaps to restore them to health. These rites are distinct from those in the second part of this book, which are provided to comfort and strengthen a Christian in the passage from this life.

43   The concern that Christ showed for the bodily and spiritual welfare of those who are ill is continued by the Church in its ministry to the sick. This ministry is the common responsibility of all Christians, who should visit the sick, remember them in prayer, and celebrate the sacraments with them. The family and friends of the sick, doctors and others who care for them, and priests with pastoral responsibilities have a particular share in this ministry of comfort. Through words of encouragement and faith they can help the sick to unite themselves with the sufferings of Christ for the good of God's people.

      Remembrance of the sick is especially appropriate at common worship on the Lord's Day, during the general intercessions at Mass and in the intercessions at Morning Prayer and Evening Prayer. Family members and those who are dedicated to the care of the sick should be remembered on these occasions as well.

44   Priests have the special task of preparing the sick to celebrate the sacrament of penance (individually or in a communal celebration), to receive the eucharist frequently if their condition permits, and to celebrate the sacrament of anointing at the appropriate time. During this preparation it will be especially helpful if the sick person, the priest, and the family become accustomed to praying together. The priest should provide leadership to those who assist him in the care of the sick, especially deacons and other ministers of the eucharist.

The words "priest," "deacon," and "minister" are used advisedly. Only in those rites which must be celebrated by a priest is the word "priest" used in the rubrics (that is, the sacrament of penance, the sacrament of the anointing of the sick, the celebration of viaticum within Mass). Whenever it is clear that, in the absence of a priest, a deacon may preside at a particular rite, the words "priest or deacon" are used in the rubrics. Whenever another minister is permitted to celebrate a rite in the absence of a priest or deacon, the word "minister" is used in the rubrics, even though in many cases the rite will be celebrated by a priest or deacon.

45   The pastoral care of the sick should be suited to the nature and length of the illness. An illness of short duration in which the full recovery of health is a possibility requires a more intensive ministry, whereas illness of a longer duration which may be a prelude to death requires a more extensive ministry. An awareness of the attitudes and emotional states which these different situations engender in the sick is indispensable to the development of an appropriate ministry.

VISITS TO THE SICK

46   Those who visit the sick should help them to pray, sharing with them the word of God proclaimed in the assembly from

which their sickness has separated them. As the occasion permits, prayer drawn from the psalms or from other prayers or litanies may be added to the word of God. Care should be taken to prepare for a future visit during which the sick will receive the eucharist.

VISITS TO A SICK CHILD

47   What has already been said about visiting the sick and praying with them (see no. 46) applies also in visits to a sick child. Every effort should be made to know the child and to accommodate the care in keeping with the age and comprehension of the child. In these circumstances the minister should also be particularly concerned to help the child's family.

48   If it is appropriate, the priest may discuss with the parents the possibility of preparing and celebrating with the child the sacraments of initiation (baptism, confirmation, eucharist). The priest may baptize and confirm the child (see *Rite of Confirmation*, no. 7b). To complete the process of initiation, the child should also receive first communion. (If the child is a proper subject for confirmation, then he or she may receive first communion in accordance with the practice of the Church.) There is no reason to delay this, especially if the illness is likely to be a long one.

49   Throughout the illness the minister should ensure that the child receives communion frequently, making whatever adaptations seem necessary in the rite for communion of the sick (Chapter III).

50   The child is to be anointed if he or she has sufficient use of reason to be strengthened by the sacrament of anointing. The rites provided (Chapter IV) are to be used and adapted.

COMMUNION OF THE SICK

51   Because the sick are prevented from celebrating the eucharist with the rest of the community, the most important visits are those during which they receive holy communion. In receiving the body and blood of Christ, the sick are united sacramentally to the Lord and are reunited with the eucharistic community from which illness has separated them.

ANOINTING OF THE SICK

52   The priest should be especially concerned for those whose health has been seriously impaired by illness or old age. He will offer them a new sign of hope: the laying on of hands and the anointing of the sick accompanied by the prayer of faith (James 5:14). Those who receive this sacrament in the faith of the Church will find it a true sign of comfort and support in time of trial. It will work to overcome the sickness, if this is God's will.

53   Some types of mental sickness are now classified as serious. Those who are judged to have a serious mental illness and who would be strengthened by the sacrament may be anointed (see no. 5). The anointing may be repeated in accordance with the conditions for other kinds of serious illness (see no. 9).

Visits to the Sick

INTRODUCTION

I was sick, and you visited me.

54   The prayers contained in this chapter follow the common pattern of reading, response, prayer, and blessing. This pattern is provided as an example of what can be done and may be adapted as necessary. The minister may wish to invite those present to prepare for the reading from Scripture, perhaps by a brief introduction or through a moment of silence. The laying on of hands may be added by the priest, if appropriate, after the blessing is given.

55   The sick should be encouraged to pray when they are alone or with their families, friends, or those who care for them. Their prayer should be drawn primarily from Scripture. The sick person and others may help to plan the celebration, for example, by choosing the prayers and readings. Those making these choices should keep in mind the condition of the sick person.

The passages found in this chapter and those included in Part III speak of the mystery of human suffering in the words, works, and life of Christ. Occasionally, for example, on the Lord's Day, the sick may feel more involved in the worship of the community from which they are separated if the readings used are those assigned for that day in the lectionary. Prayers may also be drawn from the psalms or from other prayers or litanies. The sick should be helped in making this form of prayer, and the minister should always be ready to pray with them.

56   The minister should encourage the sick person to offer his or her sufferings in union with Christ and to join in prayer for the Church and the world. Some examples of particular intentions which may be suggested to the sick person are: for peace in the world; for a deepening of the life of the Spirit in the local Church; for the pope and the bishops; for people suffering in a particular disaster.

VISITS TO THE SICK

READING

57   *The word of God is proclaimed by one of those present or by the minister. An appropriate reading from Part III or one of the following readings may be used:*

A   Acts of the Apostles 3:1–10

In the name of Jesus and the power of his Church, there is salvation—even liberation from sickness.

B   Matthew 8:14–17

Jesus fulfills the prophetic figure of the servant of God taking upon himself and relieving the sufferings of God's people.

RESPONSE

58   *A brief period of silence may be observed after the reading of the word of God. An appropriate psalm from Part III or one of the following psalms may be used:*

A   Psalm 102

R. O Lord, hear my prayer and let my cry come to you.

O LORD, hear my prayer,
       and let my cry come to you.

Hide not your face from me
    in the day of my distress.
Incline your ear to me;
    in the day when I call, answer me speedily.

R. *O Lord, hear my prayer and*
let my cry come to you.

He has broken down my strength in the way;
    he has cut short my days.
        I say: O my God,
Take me not hence in the midst of my days;
    through all generations your years endure.

R. *O Lord, hear my prayer and*
let my cry come to you.

Of old you established the earth,
    and the heavens are the work of your hands.
They shall perish, but you remain
    though all of them grow old like a garment.
Like clothing you change them, and they are changed,
    but you are the same,
and your years have no end.

R. *O Lord, hear my prayer and*
let my cry come to you.

Let this be written for the generation to come,
    and let his future creatures praise the LORD:

"The LORD looked down from his holy height,
     from heaven he beheld the earth,
To hear the groaning of the prisoners,
     to release those doomed to die."

R. *O Lord, hear my prayer and*
let my cry come to you.

B   *Psalm 27*

R. *The Lord is my light and my salvation.*

The LORD is my light and my salvation;
     whom should I fear?
The LORD is my life's refuge;
     of whom should I be afraid?

R. *The Lord is my light and my salvation.*

One thing I ask of the LORD;
     this I seek:
To dwell in the house of the LORD
     all the days of my life
That I may gaze on the loveliness of the LORD
     and contemplate his temple.

R. *The Lord is my light and my salvation.*

For he will hide me in his abode
     in the day of trouble,

He will conceal me in the shelter of his tent,
      he will set me high upon a rock.

R. *The Lord is my light and my salvation.*

*The minister may then give a brief explanation of the reading, applying it to the
needs of the sick person and those who are looking after him or her.*

THE LORD'S PRAYER

59   *The minister introduces the Lord's Prayer in these or similar words:*

Now let us offer together the prayer our Lord Jesus
Christ taught us:

All say:

Our Father . . .

CONCLUDING PRAYER

60   *The minister says a concluding prayer. One of the following may be used:*

A

Father,
your Son accepted our sufferings
to teach us the virtue of patience in human illness.
Hear the prayers we offer for our sick brother/sister.
May all who suffer pain, illness, or disease realize
that they have been chosen to be saints and know

that they are joined to Christ in his suffering for the
salvation of the world.

We ask this through Christ our Lord.
R. Amen.

B

All-powerful and ever-living God,
the lasting health of all who believe in you,
hear us as we ask your loving help for the sick;
restore their health,
that they may again offer joyful thanks
        in your Church.

Grant this through Christ our Lord.
R. Amen.

C

All-powerful and ever-living God,
we find security in your forgiveness.
Give us serenity and peace of mind;
may we rejoice in your gifts of kindness
and use them always for your glory and our good.

We ask this in the name of Jesus the Lord.
R. Amen.

BLESSING

61 *The minister may give a blessing. One of the following may be used:*

A

All praise and glory is yours, Lord our God,
for you have called us to serve you in love.
Bless N.
so that he/she may bear this illness
in union with your Son's obedient suffering.
Restore him/her to health,
and lead him/her to glory.

We ask this through Christ our Lord.
R. Amen.

B

For an elderly person

All praise and glory are yours, Lord our God,
for you have called us to serve you in love.
Bless all who have grown old in your service
and give N. strength and courage
to continue to follow Jesus your Son.

We ask this through Christ our Lord.
R. Amen.

A minister who is not a priest or deacon invokes God's blessing and makes the sign of the cross on himself or herself, while saying:

May the Lord bless us,
protect us from all evil,
and bring us to everlasting life.
R. Amen.

The minister may then trace the sign of the cross on the sick person's forehead.

Visits To A Sick Child

INTRODUCTION

Let the children come to me; do not keep them back from me.

62   The following readings, prayers, and blessings will help the minister to pray with sick children and their families. They are provided as an example of what can be done and may be adapted as necessary. The minister may wish to invite those present to prepare for the reading from Scripture, perhaps by a brief introduction or through a moment of silence.

63   If the child does not already know the minister, the latter should seek to establish a friendly and easy relationship with the child. Therefore, the greeting which begins the visit should be an informal one.

64   The minister should help sick children to understand that the sick are very special in the eyes of God because they are suffering as Christ suffered and because they can offer their sufferings for the salvation of the world.

65   In praying with the sick child the minister chooses, together with the child and the family if possible, suitable elements of common prayer in the form of a brief liturgy of the word. This may consist of a reading from Scripture, simple one-line prayers taken from Scripture which can be repeated by the child, other familiar prayers such as the Lord's Prayer, the Hail Mary, litanies, or a simple form of the general intercessions. The laying on of hands may be added by the priest, if appropriate, after the child has been blessed.

READING

66   *One of the following readings may be used for a brief liturgy of the word. Other readings may be chosen, for example: Mark 5:21–23, 35–43, Jesus raises the daughter of Jairus and gives her back to her parents; Mark 9:14–27, Jesus cures a boy and gives him back to his father; Luke 7:11–15, Jesus raises a young man, the only son of his mother, and gives him back to her; John 4:46–53, Jesus gives his second sign by healing an official's son. In addition, other stories concerning the Lord's healing ministry may be found suitable, especially if told with the simplicity and clarity of one of the children's versions of Scripture.*

A   Mark 9:33–37

Jesus proposes the child as the ideal of those who would enter the kingdom.

B   Mark 10:13–16

Jesus welcomes the children and lays hands on them.

RESPONSE

67   *After the reading of the word of God, time may be set apart for silent reflection if the child is capable of this form of prayer. The minister should also explain the meaning of the reading to those present, adapting it to their circumstances.*

The minister may then help the child and the family to respond to the word of God. The following short responsory may be used:

Jesus, come to me.

—*Jesus, come to me.*

Jesus, put your hand on me.

—*Jesus, put your hand on me.*

Jesus, bless me.

—*Jesus, bless me.*

THE LORD'S PRAYER

68   *The minister introduces the Lord's Prayer in these or similar words:*

Let us pray to the Father using those words which Jesus himself used:

All say:

Our Father . . .

CONCLUDING PRAYER

69   *The minister says a concluding prayer. One of the following may be used.*

A
God of love,
ever caring,
ever strong,
stand by us in our time of need.

Watch over your child **N.** who is sick,
look after him/her in every danger,
and grant him/her your healing and peace.

We ask this in the name of Jesus the Lord.
R. Amen.

B

Father,
in your love
you gave us Jesus
to help us rise triumphant over grief and pain.

Look on your child *N.* who is sick
and see in his/her sufferings those of your Son.

Grant *N.* a share in the strength you granted your Son
that he/she too may be a sign
of your goodness, kindness, and loving care.

We ask this in the name of Jesus the Lord.
R. Amen.

BLESSING

*70   The minister makes a sign of the cross on the child's forehead, saying one
of the following:*

A

N., when you were baptized,
you were marked with the cross of Jesus.
I (we) make this cross ✚ on your forehead
and ask the Lord to bless you,
and restore you to health.
R. Amen.

B

All praise and glory is yours, heavenly God,
for you have called us to serve you in love.
Have mercy on us and listen to our prayer
as we ask you to help N.

Bless ✚ your beloved child,
and restore him/her to health
in the name of Jesus the Lord.

R. Amen.

Each one present may in turn trace the sign of the cross on the child's forehead, in silence.

A minister who is not a priest or deacon concludes as described in no. 61.

Communion of the Sick

INTRODUCTION

Whoever eats this bread will live for ever.

71   This chapter contains two rites: one for use when communion can be celebrated in the context of a liturgy of the word; the other, a brief communion rite for use in more restrictive circumstances, such as in hospitals.

72   Priests with pastoral responsibilities should see to it that the sick or aged, even though not seriously ill or in danger of death, are given every opportunity to receive the eucharist frequently, even daily, especially during the Easter season. They may receive communion at any hour. Those who care for the sick may receive communion with them, in accord with the usual norms. To provide frequent communion for the sick, it may be necessary to ensure that the community has a sufficient number of ministers of communion. The communion minister should wear attire appropriate to this ministry.

The sick person and others may help to plan the celebration, for example, by choosing the prayers and readings. Those making these choices should keep in mind the condition of the sick person. The readings and the homily should help those present to reach a deeper understanding of the mystery of human suffering in relation to the paschal mystery of Christ.

73   The faithful who are ill are deprived of their rightful and accustomed place in the eucharistic community. In bringing communion to them the minister of communion represents Christ and manifests faith and charity on behalf of the whole community toward those who cannot be present at the eucharist. For the sick the reception of communion is not only a privilege

but also a sign of support and concern shown by the Christian community for its members who are ill.

The links between the community's eucharistic celebration, especially on the Lord's Day, and the communion of the sick are intimate and manifold. Besides remembering the sick in the general intercessions at Mass, those present should be reminded occasionally of the significance of communion in the lives of those who are ill: union with Christ in his struggle with evil, his prayer for the world, and his love for the Father, and union with the community from which they are separated.

The obligation to visit and comfort those who cannot take part in the eucharistic assembly may be clearly demonstrated by taking communion to them from the community's eucharistic celebration. This symbol of unity between the community and its sick members has the deepest significance on the Lord's Day, the special day of the eucharistic assembly.

74   When the eucharist is brought to the sick, it should be carried in a pyx or small closed container. Those who are with the sick should be asked to prepare a table covered with a linen cloth upon which the blessed sacrament will be placed. Lighted candles are prepared and, where it is customary, a vessel of holy water. Care should be taken to make the occasion special and joyful.

Sick people who are unable to receive communion under the form of bread may receive it under the form of wine alone. If the wine is consecrated at a Mass not celebrated in the presence of the sick person, the blood of the Lord is kept in a properly covered vessel and is placed in the tabernacle after communion. The precious blood should be carried to the sick in a vessel which is closed in such a way as to eliminate all danger of spilling. If some of the precious blood remains, it should be consumed by the minister, who should also see to it that the vessel is properly purified.

75   If the sick wish to celebrate the sacrament of penance, it is preferable that the priest make himself available for this during a previous visit.

76   If it is necessary to celebrate the sacrament of penance during the rite of communion, it takes the place of the penitential rite.

COMMUNION IN ORDINARY CIRCUMSTANCES

77   If possible, provision should be made to celebrate Mass in the homes of the sick, with their families and friends gathered around them. The Ordinary determines the conditions and requirements for such celebrations.

COMMUNION IN A HOSPITAL OR INSTITUTION

78   There will be situations, particularly in large institutions with many communicants, when the minister should consider alternative means so that the rite of communion of the sick is not diminished to the absolute minimum. In such cases the following alternatives should be considered: (a) where possible, the residents or patients may be gathered in groups in one or more areas; (b) additional ministers of communion may assist.

When it is not possible to celebrate the full rite, the rite for communion in a hospital or institution may be used. If it is convenient, however, the minister may add elements from the rite for ordinary circumstances, for example, a Scripture reading.

79   The rite begins with the recitation of the eucharistic antiphon in the church, the hospital chapel, or the first room visited. Then the minister gives communion to the sick in their individual rooms.

80   The concluding prayer may be said in the church, the hospital chapel, or the last room visited. No blessing is given.

COMMUNION IN ORDINARY CIRCUMSTANCES

INTRODUCTORY RITES

Greeting

81   *The minister greets the sick person and the others present. One of the following may be used:*

A

The peace of the Lord be with you always.
R. And also with you.

B

Peace be with you (this house) and with all who
live here.
R. And also with you.

C

The grace of our Lord Jesus Christ and the love of
God and the fellowship of the Holy Spirit be with
you all.
R. And also with you.

D

The grace and peace of God our Father and the Lord
Jesus Christ be with you.

R. *And also with you.*

*The minister then places the blessed sacrament on the table and all join in
adoration.*

PENITENTIAL RITE

83   *The minister invites the sick person and all present to join in the
penitential rite, using these or similar words:*

A

My brothers and sisters, to prepare ourselves for this
celebration, let us call to mind our sins.

B

My brothers and sisters, let us turn with confidence
to the Lord and ask his forgiveness for all our sins.

*After a brief period of silence, the penitential rite continues, using one of the
following:*

A

Lord Jesus, you healed the sick:
Lord, have mercy.

R. *Lord, have mercy.*

Lord Jesus, you forgave sinners:
Christ, have mercy.
R. *Christ, have mercy.*

Lord Jesus, you give us yourself to heal us
        and bring us strength:
Lord, have mercy.
R. *Lord, have mercy.*

B

All say:

I confess to almighty God,
and to you, my brothers and sisters,
that I have sinned through my own fault

They strike their breast.
in my thoughts and in my words,
in what I have done,
and in what I have failed to do;
and I ask blessed Mary, ever virgin,
all the angels and saints,
and you, my brothers and sisters,
to pray for me to the Lord our God.

The minister concludes the penitential rite with the following:
May almighty God have mercy on us,
forgive us our sins,
and bring us to everlasting life.
R. *Amen.*

LITURGY OF THE WORD
Reading

84   *The word of God is proclaimed by one of those present or by the minister.*
An appropriate reading from Part III or one of the following readings may
be used:

A *John 6:51*
B *John 6:54–58*
C *John 14:6*
D *John 15:5*
E *John 4:16*

Response

85   *A brief period of silence may be observed after the reading of the word*
of God.

The minister may then give a brief explanation of the reading, applying it to the
needs of the sick person and those who are looking after him or her.

GENERAL INTERCESSIONS

86   *The general intercessions may be said. With a brief introduction the*
minister invites all those present to pray. After the intentions the minister says the
concluding prayer. It is desirable that the intentions be announced by someone
other than the minister.

LITURGY OF HOLY COMMUNION
The Lord's Prayer

87   *The minister introduces the Lord's Prayer in these or similar words:*

A

Now let us pray as Christ the Lord has taught us:

B

And now let us pray with confidence as Christ our
Lord commanded:

All say:

Our Father . . .

Communion

88   *The minister shows the eucharistic bread to those present, saying:*

A

This is the bread of life.
Taste and see that the Lord is good.

B

This is the Lamb of God
who takes away the sins of the world.
Happy are those who are called to his supper.

The sick person and all who are to receive communion say:

Lord, I am not worthy to receive you,
but only say the word and I shall be healed.

The minister goes to the sick person and, showing the blessed sacrament, says:

The body of Christ.

The sick person answers: "Amen," and receives communion.

Then the minister says:

The blood of Christ.

The sick person answers: "Amen," and receives communion.
Others present who wish to receive communion then do so in the usual way.

After the conclusion of the rite, the minister cleanses the vessel as usual.

Silent Prayer

89   *Then a period of silence may be observed.*

Prayer after Communion

90   *The minister says a concluding prayer. One of the following may be used:*

Let us pray.

Pause for silent prayer, if this has not preceded.

A

God our Father,
you have called us to share the one bread
      and one cup
and so become one in Christ.

Help us to live in him
that we may bear fruit,
rejoicing that he has redeemed the world.

We ask this through Christ our Lord.
R. Amen.

B

All-powerful God,
we thank you for the nourishment you give us
through your holy gift.

Pour out your Spirit upon us
and in the strength of this food from heaven
keep us single-minded in your service.

We ask this in the name of Jesus the Lord.
R. *Amen.*

C
All-powerful and ever-living God,
may the body and blood of Christ your Son
be for our brother/sister N.
a lasting remedy for body and soul.

We ask this through Christ our Lord.
R. *Amen.*

CONCLUDING RITE
Blessing

91   *A minister who is not a priest or deacon invokes God's blessing and*
makes the sign of the cross on himself or herself, while saying:

A
May the Lord bless us,
protect us from all evil,
and bring us to everlasting life.
R. *Amen.*

B

May the almighty and merciful God bless and
      protect us,
the Father, and the Son, ✝ and the Holy Spirit.
R. Amen.

COMMUNION IN A HOSPITAL OR INSTITUTION

INTRODUCTORY RITE

Antiphon

92   *The rite may begin in the church, the hospital chapel, or the first room, where the minister says one of the following antiphons:*

A

How holy this feast
in which Christ is our food:
his passion is recalled;
grace fills our hearts;
and we receive a pledge of the glory to come.

B

How gracious you are, Lord:
your gift of bread from heaven
reveals a Father's love and brings us perfect joy.
You fill the hungry with good things
and send the rich away empty.

C

I am the living bread
come down from heaven.
If you eat this bread
you will live for ever.

The bread I will give is my flesh
for the life of the world.

*If it is customary, the minister may be accompanied by a person carrying
a candle.*

LITURGY OF HOLY COMMUNION
Greeting

93   *On entering each room, the minister may use one of the
following greetings:*

A

The peace of the Lord be with you always.
R. *And also with you.*

B

The grace of our Lord Jesus Christ and the love of
God and the fellowship of the Holy Spirit be with
you all.
R. *And also with you.*

*The minister then places the blessed sacrament on the table, and all join
in adoration.*

*If there is time and it seems desirable, the minister may proclaim
a scripture reading from those found in no. 84 or those appearing in Part III.*

The Lord's Prayer

94   *When circumstances permit (for example, when there are not many rooms
to visit), the minister is encouraged to lead the sick in the Lord's Prayer. The
minister introduces the Lord's Prayer in these or similar words:*

A

Jesus taught us to call God our Father, and so we
have the courage to say:

B

Now let us pray as Christ the Lord has taught us:
All say:
Our Father . . .

Communion

95   *The minister shows the eucharistic bread to those present, saying:*

A

This is the Lamb of God
who takes away the sins of the world.
Happy are those who hunger and thirst,
for they shall be satisfied.

B

This it the bread of life,
Taste and see that the Lord is good.

The sick person and all who are to receive communion say:

Lord, I am not worthy to receive you,
but only say the word and I shall be healed.

The minister goes to the sick person and, showing the blessed sacrament, says:

The body of Christ.

The sick person answers: "Amen," and receives communion.

Then the minister says:

The blood of Christ.

The sick person answers: "Amen," and receives communion.

Others present who wish to receive communion then do so in the usual way.

CONCLUDING RITE
Concluding Prayer

96   *The concluding prayer may be said either in the last room visited, in the church, or chapel. One of the following may be used:*

Let us pray.

Pause for silent prayer.

A
God our Father,
you have called us to share the one bread
        and one cup
and so become one in Christ.

Help us to live in him
that we may bear fruit,
rejoicing that he has redeemed the world.

We ask this through Christ our Lord.
R. Amen.

B

All-powerful and ever-living God,
may the body and blood of Christ your Son
be for our brothers and sisters
a lasting remedy for body and soul.
We ask this through Christ our Lord.
R. Amen.

C

All-powerful God,
we thank you for the nourishment you give us
through your holy gift.

Pour out your Spirit upon us
and in the strength of this food from heaven
keep us single-minded in your service.

We ask this in the name of Jesus the Lord.
R. Amen.

The blessing is omitted and the minister cleanses the vessel as usual.

Pastoral Care of the Dying

INTRODUCTION

When we were baptized in Christ Jesus we were baptized into his death . . . so that as Christ was raised from the dead by the Father's glory, we too might live a new life.

161   The rites in Part II of *Pastoral Care of the Sick: Rites of Anointing and Viaticum* are used by the Church to comfort and strengthen a dying Christian in the passage from this life. The ministry to the dying places emphasis on trust in the Lord's promise of eternal life rather than on the struggle against illness which is characteristic of the pastoral care of the sick.

    The first three chapters of Part II provide for those situations in which time is not a pressing concern and the rites can be celebrated fully and properly. These are to be clearly distinguished from the rites contained in Chapter Eight, "Rites for Exceptional Circumstances," which provide for the emergency situations sometimes encountered in the ministry to the dying.

162   Priests with pastoral responsibilities are to direct the efforts of the family and friends as well as other ministers of the local Church in the care of the dying. They should ensure that all are familiar with the rites provided here.

    The words "priest," "deacon," and "minister" are used advisedly. Only in those rites which must be celebrated by a priest is the word "priest" used in the rubrics (that is, the sacrament of penance, the sacrament of the anointing of the sick, the celebration of viaticum within Mass). Whenever it is clear that, in the absence of a priest, a deacon may preside at a particular rite, the words "priest or deacon," are used in the rubrics. Whenever another minister is permitted to celebrate a rite in the absence of a priest or deacon, the word "minister" is used in the rubrics, even though in many cases the rite will be celebrated by a priest or deacon.

163   The Christian community has a continuing responsibility to pray for and with the person who is dying. Through its sacramental ministry to the dying the community helps Christians to embrace death in mysterious union with the crucified and risen Lord, who awaits them in the fullness of life.

CELEBRATION OF VIATICUM

164   A rite for viaticum within Mass and another for viaticum outside Mass are provided. If possible, viaticum should take place within the full eucharistic celebration, with the family, friends, and other members of the Christian community taking part. The rite for viaticum outside Mass is used when the full eucharistic celebration cannot take place. Again, if it is possible, others should take part.

COMMENDATION OF THE DYING

165   The second chapter of Part II contains a collection of prayers for the spiritual comfort of the Christian who is close to death. These prayers are traditionally called the commendation of the dying to God and are to be used according to the circumstances of each case.

PRAYERS FOR THE DEAD

166   A chapter has also been provided to assist a minister who has been called to attend a person who is already dead. A priest is not to administer the sacrament of anointing. Instead, he should pray for the dead person, using prayers such as those which appear in this chapter. He may find it necessary to explain

to the family of the person who is dead that sacraments are celebrated for the living, not for the dead, and that the dead are effectively helped by the prayers of the living.

RITES FOR EXCEPTIONAL CIRCUMSTANCES

167 Chapter Eight, "Rites for Exceptional Circumstances," contains rites which should be celebrated with a person who has suddenly been placed in proximate or immediate danger of death. They are for emergency circumstances and should be used only when such pressing conditions exist.

CARE OF A DYING CHILD

168 In its ministry to the dying the Church must also respond to the difficult circumstances of a dying child. Although no specific rites appear in Part II for the care of a dying child, these notes are provided to help bring into focus the various aspects of this ministry.

169 When parents learn that their child is dying, they are often bewildered and hurt. In their love for their son or daughter, they may be beset by temptations and doubts and find themselves asking: Why is God taking this child from us? How have we sinned or failed that God would punish us in this way? Why is this innocent child being hurt?

Under these trying circumstances, much of the Church's ministry will be directed to the parents and family. While pain and suffering in an innocent child are difficult for others to bear, the Church helps the parents and family to accept what God has allowed to happen. It should be understood by all beforehand that this process of acceptance will probably extend beyond the death of the child. The concern of the Christian community should continue as long as necessary.

Concern for the child must be equal to that for the family. Those who deal with dying children observe that their faith matures rapidly. Though young children often seem to accept death more easily than adults, they will often experience a surprisingly mature anguish because of the pain which they see in their families.

170   At such a time, it is important for members of the Christian community to come to the support of the child and the family by prayer, visits, and other forms of assistance. Those who have lost children of their own have a ministry of consolation and support to the family. Hospital personnel (doctors, nurses, aides) should also be prepared to exercise a special role with the child as caring adults. Priests and deacons bear particular responsibility for overseeing all these elements of the Church's pastoral ministry. The minister should invite members of the community to use their individual gifts in this work of communal care and concern.

171   By conversation and brief services of readings and prayers, the minister may help the parents and family to see that their child is being called ahead of them to enter the kingdom and joy of the Lord. The period when the child is dying can become a special time of renewal and prayer for the family and close friends. The minister should help them to see that the child's sufferings are united to those of Jesus for the salvation of the whole world.

172   If it is appropriate, the priest should discuss with the parents the possibility of preparing and celebrating with the child the sacraments of initiation (baptism, confirmation, eucharist). The priest may baptize and confirm the child (see *Rite of Confirmation*, no. 7b). To complete the process of initiation, the child should also receive first communion.

According to the circumstances, some of these rites may be celebrated by a deacon or layperson. So that the child and family may receive full benefit from them, these rites are normally celebrated over a period of time. In this case, the minister should use the usual rites, that is, the *Rite of Baptism for Children*, the *Rite of Confirmation*, and if suitable, the *Rite of Penance*. Similarly, if time allows, the usual rites for anointing and viaticum should be celebrated.

173   If sudden illness or an accident has placed an uninitiated child in proximate danger of death, the minister uses "Christian Initiation for the Dying," adapting it for use with a child.

174   For an initiated child or a child lacking only the sacrament of confirmation, who is in proximate danger of death, the "Continuous Rite of Penance, Anointing, and Viaticum" may be used and adapted to the understanding of the child. If death is imminent it should be remembered that viaticum rather than anointing is the sacrament for the dying.

CELEBRATION OF VIATICUM

INTRODUCTION

I am going to prepare a place for you; I shall come back and take you with me.

175   This chapter contains a rite for viaticum within Mass and a rite for viaticum outside Mass. The celebration of the eucharist as viaticum, food for the passage through death to eternal life, is the sacrament proper to the dying Christian. It is the completion and crown of the Christian life on this earth, signifying that the Christian follows the Lord to eternal glory and the banquet of the heavenly kingdom.

The sacrament of the anointing of the sick should be celebrated at the beginning of a serious illness. Viaticum, celebrated when death is close, will then be better understood as the last sacrament of Christian life.

176   Priests and other ministers entrusted with the spiritual care of the sick should do everything they can to ensure that those in proximate danger of death receive the body and blood of Christ as viaticum. At the earliest opportunity, the necessary preparation should be given to the dying person, family, and others who may take part.

177   Whenever it is possible, the dying Christian should be able to receive viaticum within Mass. In this way he or she shares fully, during the final moments of this life, in the eucharistic sacrifice, which proclaims the Lord's own passing through death to life. However, circumstances, such as confinement to a hospital ward or the very emergency which makes death imminent, may frequently make the complete eucharistic celebration impossible.

In this case, the rite for viaticum outside Mass is appropriate. The minister should wear attire appropriate to this ministry.

178 Because the celebration of viaticum ordinarily takes place in the limited circumstances of the home, a hospital, or other institution, the simplifications of the rite for Masses in small gatherings may be appropriate. Depending on the condition of the dying person, every effort should be made to involve him or her, the family, friends, and other members of the local community in the planning and celebration. Appropriate readings, prayers, and songs will help to foster the full participation of all. Because of this concern for participation, the minister should ensure that viaticum is celebrated while the dying person is still able to take part and respond.

179 A distinctive feature of the celebration of viaticum, whether within or outside Mass, is the renewal of the baptismal profession of faith by the dying person. This occurs after the homily and replaces the usual form of the profession of faith. Through the baptismal profession at the end of earthly life, the one who is dying uses the language of his or her initial commitment, which is renewed each Easter and on other occasions in the Christian life. In the context of viaticum, it is a renewal and fulfillment of initiation into the Christian mysteries, baptism leading to the eucharist.

180 The rites for viaticum within and outside Mass may include the sign of peace. The minister and all who are present embrace the dying Christian. In this and in other parts of the celebration the sense of leave-taking need not be concealed or denied, but the joy of Christian hope, which is the comfort and strength of the one near death, should also be evident.

181 As an indication that the reception of the eucharist by the dying Christian is a pledge of resurrection and food for the passage through death, the special words proper to viaticum are added: "May the Lord Jesus Christ protect you and lead you to eternal life." The dying person and all who are present may receive communion under both kinds. The sign of communion is more complete when received in this manner because it expresses more fully and clearly the nature of the eucharist as a meal, one which prepares all who take part in it for the heavenly banquet (see the *General Instruction of the Roman Missal*, no. 240).

The minister should choose the manner of giving communion under both kinds which is suitable in the particular case. If the wine is consecrated at a Mass not celebrated in the presence of the sick person, the blood of the Lord is kept in a properly covered vessel and is placed in the tabernacle after communion. The precious blood should be carried to the sick person in a vessel which is closed in such a way as to eliminate all danger of spilling. If some of the precious blood remains after communion, it should be consumed by the minister, who should also see to it that the vessel is properly purified.

The sick who are unable to receive under the form of bread may receive under the form of wine alone. If the wine is consecrated at a Mass not celebrated in the presence of the sick person, the instructions given above are followed.

182 In addition to these elements of the rites which are to be given greater stress, special texts are provided for the general intercessions or litany and the final solemn blessing.

183 It often happens that a person who has received the eucharist as viaticum lingers in a grave condition or at the point of death for a period of days or longer. In these circumstances he or she should be given the opportunity to receive the eucharist

as viaticum on successive days, frequently if not daily. This may take place during or outside Mass as particular conditions permit. The rite may be simplified according to the condition of the one who is dying.

VIATICUM WITHIN MASS

184   When viaticum is received within Mass, the ritual Mass for Viaticum or the Mass of the Holy Eucharist may be celebrated. The priest wears white vestments. The readings may be taken from *The Lectionary for Mass* (second edition, nos. 796–800), unless the dying person and those involved with the priest in planning the liturgy choose other readings from Scripture.

A ritual Mass is not permitted during the Easter triduum, on the solemnities of Christmas, Epiphany, Ascension, Pentecost, Corpus Christi, or on a solemnity which is a holy day of obligation. On these occasions, the texts and readings are taken from the Mass of the day. Although the Mass for Viaticum or the Mass of the Holy Eucharist are also excluded on the Sundays of Advent, Lent, and the Easter season, on solemnities, Ash Wednesday, and the weekdays of Holy Week, one of the readings may be taken from the biblical texts indicated above. The special form of the final blessing may be used and, at the discretion of the priest, the apostolic pardon may be added.

185   If the dying person wishes to celebrate the sacrament of penance, it is preferable that the priest make himself available for this during a previous visit. If this is not possible, the sacrament of penance may be celebrated before Mass begins (see Appendix, p. 372).

VIATICUM OUTSIDE MASS

186   Although viaticum celebrated in the context of the full eucharistic celebration is always preferable, when it is not

possible the rite for viaticum outside Mass is appropriate. This rite includes some of the elements of the Mass, especially a brief liturgy of the word. Depending on the circumstances and the condition of the dying person, this rite should also be a communal celebration. Every effort should be made to involve the dying person, family, friends, and members of the local community in the planning and celebration. The manner of celebration and the elements of the rite which are used should be accommodated to those present and the nearness of death.

187   If the dying person wishes to celebrate the sacrament of penance and this cannot take place during a previous visit, it should be celebrated before the rite of viaticum begins, especially if others are present. Alternatively, it may be celebrated during the rite of viaticum, replacing the penitential rite. At the discretion of the priest, the apostolic pardon may be added after the penitential rite or after the sacrament of penance.

188   An abbreviated liturgy of the word, ordinarily consisting of a single biblical reading, gives the minister an opportunity to explain the word of God in relation to viaticum. The sacrament should be described as the sacred food which strengthens the Christian for the passage through death to life in sure hope of the resurrection.

VIATICUM OUTSIDE MASS

INTRODUCTORY RITES

Greeting

197   *The minister greets the sick person and the others present. The following may be used:*

A

The peace of the Lord be with you always.

R. And also with you.

B

Peace be with you (this house) and with all who
live here.

R. And also with you.

C

The grace of our Lord Jesus Christ and the love of
God and the fellowship of the Holy Spirit be with
you all.

R. And also with you.

D

The grace and peace of God our Father and the Lord
Jesus Christ be with you.

R. And also with you.

The minister then places the blessed sacrament on the table, and all join in adoration.

Instruction

199   Afterward the minister addresses those present, using the following instruction or one better suited to the sick person's condition:

My brothers and sisters, before our Lord Jesus Christ passed from this world to return to the Father, he left us the sacrament of his body and blood. When the hour comes for us to pass from this life and join him, he strengthens us with this food for our journey and comforts us by this pledge of our resurrection.

Penitential Rite

200   The minister invites the sick person and all present to join in the penitential rite, using these or similar words:

A

My brothers and sisters, to prepare ourselves for this celebration, let us call to mind our sins.

B

My brothers and sisters, let us turn with confidence to the Lord and ask his forgiveness for all our sins.

After a brief period of silence, the penitential rite continues using one of the following prayers.

A   *All say:*

I confess to almighty God,
and to you, my brothers and sisters,
that I have sinned through my own fault

They strike their breast.

in my thoughts and in my words,
in what I have done,
and in what I have failed to do;
and I ask blessed Mary, every virgin,
all the angels and saints,
and you, my brothers and sisters,
to pray for me to the Lord our God.

B

By your paschal mystery
        you have won for us salvation:
Lord, have mercy.
R. *Lord, have mercy.*

You renew among us now
        the wonders of your passion:
Christ, have mercy.
R. *Christ, have mercy.*

When we receive your body,
you share with us your paschal sacrifice:
Lord, have mercy.
R. *Lord, have mercy.*

The minister concludes the penitential rite with the following:

May almighty God have mercy us,
forgive us our sins,
and bring us to everlasting life.
R. Amen.

LITURGY OF THE WORD

Reading

202   *The word of God is proclaimed by one of those present or by the minister.*
An appropriate reading from Part III or one of the following may be used:

A John 6:54–55
B John 14:23
C John 15:4
D 1 Corinthians 11:26

Homily

203   *Depending on circumstances, the minister may then give a brief*
explanation of the reading.

Baptismal Profession of Faith

204   *It is desirable that the sick person renew his or her baptismal profession*
of faith before receiving viaticum. The minister gives a brief introduction and then
asks the following questions:

N., do you believe in God, the Father almighty,
creator of heaven and earth?
R. I do.

Do you believe in Jesus Christ, his only Son, our Lord,
who was born of the Virgin Mary,

was crucified, died, and was buried,
rose from the dead,
and is now seated at the right hand of the Father?
R. I do.

Do you believe in the Holy Spirit,
the holy catholic Church, the communion of saints,
the forgiveness of sins, the resurrection of the body,
and life everlasting?
R. I do.

Litany

205   The minister may adapt or shorten the litany according to the condition of the sick person. The litany may be omitted if the sick person has made the profession of faith and appears to be tiring.

My brothers and sisters, with one heart let us call on our Savior Jesus Christ.

You loved us to the very end and gave yourself over to death in order to give us life. For our brother/sister, Lord, we pray:
R. Lord, hear our prayer.

You said to us: "All who eat my flesh and drink my blood will live for ever." For our brother/sister, Lord, we pray:
R. Lord, hear our prayer.

You invite us to join in the banquet where pain and sorrow, sadness and separation will be no more. For our brother/sister, Lord, we pray:
R. Lord, hear our prayer.

LITURGY OF VIATICUM

The Lord's Prayer

206   The minister introduces the Lord's Prayer in these words:

A

Now let us offer together the prayer our Lord Jesus
Christ taught us:

B

And now let us pray with confidence as Christ our
Lord commanded:

All say:

Our Father . . .

Communion as Viaticum

*207   The sick person and all present may receive communion under both kinds.
When the minister gives communion to the sick person, the form for viaticum
is used.*

The minister shows the eucharistic bread to those present, saying:

A

Jesus Christ is the food for our journey;
he calls us to the heavenly table.

B

This is the bread of life.
Taste and see that the Lord is good.

The sick person and all who are to receive communion say:

Lord, I am not worthy to receive you,
but only say the word and I shall be healed.

The minister goes to the sick person and, showing the blessed sacrament, says:

The body of Christ.

The sick person answers: "Amen."

Then the minister says:

The blood of Christ.

The sick person answers: "Amen."

Immediately, or after giving communion to the sick person, the minister adds:

May the Lord Jesus Christ protect you
and lead you to eternal life.
R. Amen.

Others present who wish to receive communion then do so in the usual way.

After the conclusion of the rite, the minister cleanses the vessel as usual.

Silent Prayer

208   *Then a period of silence may be observed.*

Prayer after Communion

209   *The minister says the concluding prayer.*

Let us pray.

Pause for silent prayer, if this has not preceded.

A.

God of peace,
you offer eternal healing to those who believe in you;
you have refreshed your servant N.
with food and drink from heaven:
lead him/her safely into the kingdom of light.

We ask this through Christ our Lord.
R. Amen.

B

All-powerful and ever-living God,
may the body and blood of Christ your Son
be for our brother/sister N.
a lasting remedy for body and soul.

We ask this through Christ our Lord.
R. Amen.

C

Father,
your son, Jesus Christ, is our way, our truth,
        and our life.
Look with compassion on your servant N.
who has trusted in your promises.
You have refreshed him/her with the body and blood
        of your Son:
may he/she enter your kingdom in peace.

We ask this through Christ our Lord.
R. Amen.

CONCLUDING RITES

Blessing

210   *A minister who is not a priest or deacon invokes God's blessing and makes the sign of the cross on himself or herself, while saying:*

May the Lord bless us,
protect us from all evil,
and bring us to everlasting life.
R. Amen.

Sign of Peace

211   *The minister and the others present may then give the sick person the sign of peace.*

Commendation of the Dying

INTRODUCTION

Into your hands, Lord, I commend my spirit.

212   In viaticum the dying person is united with Christ in his passage out of this world to the Father. Through the prayers for the commendation of the dying contained in this chapter, the Church helps to sustain this union until it is brought to fulfillment after death.

213   Christians have the responsibility of expressing their union in Christ by joining the dying person in prayer for God's mercy and for confidence in Christ. In particular, the presence of a priest or deacon shows more clearly that the Christian dies in the communion of the Church. He should assist the dying person and those present in the recitation of the prayers of commendation and, following death, he should lead those present in the prayer after death. If the priest or deacon is unable to be present because of other serious pastoral obligations, other members of the community should be prepared to assist with these prayers and should have the texts readily available to them.

214   The minister may choose texts from among the prayers, litanies, aspirations, psalms, and readings provided in this chapter, or others may be added. In the selection of these texts the minister should keep in mind the condition and piety of both the dying person and the members of the family who are present. The prayers are best said in a slow, quiet voice, alternating with periods of silence. If possible, the minister says one or more of

the brief prayer formulas with the dying person. These may be softly repeated two or three times.

215   These texts are intended to help the dying person, if still conscious, to face the natural human anxiety about death by imitating Christ in his patient suffering and dying. The Christian will be helped to surmount his or her fear in the hope of heavenly life and resurrection through the power of Christ, who destroyed the power of death by his own dying.

Even if the dying person is not conscious, those who are present will draw consolation from these prayers and come to a better understanding of the paschal character of Christian death. This may be visibly expressed by making the sign of the cross on the forehead of the dying person, who was first signed with the cross at baptism.

216   Immediately after death has occurred, all may kneel while one of those present leads the prayers given on nos. 221–222.

SHORT TEXTS

217   One or more of the following short texts may be recited with the dying person. If necessary, they may be softly repeated two or three times.

Romans 8:35
Who can separate us from the love of Christ?

Romans 14:8
Whether we live or die, we are the Lord's.

2 Corinthians 5:1
We have an everlasting home in heaven.

1 Thessalonians 4:17
We shall be with the Lord for ever.

1 John 3:2
We shall see God as he really is.

1 John 3:14
We have passed from death to life
because we love each other.

Psalm 25:1
To you, Lord, I lift up my soul.

Psalm 27:1
The Lord is my light and my salvation.

Psalm 27:13
I believe that I shall see the goodness of the Lord
in the land of the living.

Psalm 42:3
My soul thirsts for the living God.

Psalm 23:4
Though I walk in the shadow of death,
I will fear no evil,
for you are with me.

Matthew 25:34
Come, blessed of my Father,
says the Lord Jesus,
and take possession of the kingdom
prepared for you.

Luke 23:43
The Lord Jesus says,
today you will be with me in paradise.

John 14:2
In my Father's home
there are many dwelling places,
says the Lord Jesus.

John 14:2–3
The Lord Jesus says,
I go to prepare a place for you,
and I will come again to take you to myself.

John 17:24
I desire that where I am,
they also may be with me,
says the Lord Jesus.

John 6:40
Everyone who believes in the Son
has eternal life.

Psalm 31:5a
Into your hands, Lord,
I commend my spirit.

Acts 7:59
Lord Jesus, receive my spirit.

Holy Mary, pray for me.

Saint Joseph, pray for me.

Jesus, Mary, and Joseph,
assist me in my last agony.

READING

218   *The word of God is proclaimed by one of those present or by the minister.
Selections from Part III or from the following readings may be used:*

A Job 19:23–27a
Job's act of faith is a model for our own; God is the God of the living.

B Psalm 23
C Psalm 25
D Psalm 91
E Psalm 121
F 1 John 4:16

G Revelation 21:1–5a, 6–7
God our Father is the God of newness of life; it is his desire that we
should come to share his life with him.

H Matthew 25:1–13
Jesus bid us be prepared for our ultimate destiny, which is eternal life.

I Luke 22:39–46
Jesus is alive to our pain and sorrow, because faithfulness to his Father's will cost him life itself.

J Luke 24:1–8
Jesus' death is witnessed by his friends.

K Luke 24:1–8
Jesus is alive; he gives us eternal life with the Father.

L John 6:37–40
Jesus will raise his own from death and give them eternal life.

M John 14:1–6, 23, 27
The love of Jesus can raise us up from the sorrow of death to the joy of eternal life.

Litany of the Saints

219   When the condition of the dying person calls for the use of brief forms of prayer, those who are present are encouraged to pray the litany of the saints— or at least some of its invocations—for him or her. Special mention may be made of the patron saints of the dying person, of the family, and of the parish. The litany may be said or sung in the usual way. Other customary prayers may also be used.

Lord, have mercy . . . . Lord, have mercy
Christ, have mercy . . . . Christ, have mercy
Lord, have mercy . . . . : . . Lord, have mercy

Holy Mary, Mother of God . . . . pray for him/her
Holy angels of God . . . . pray for him/her
Abraham, our father in faith . . . . . . pray for him/her
David, leader of God's people . . . . . pray for him/her
All holy patriarchs and prophets . . . pray for him/her

Saint John the Baptist . . . . pray for him/her
Saint Joseph . . . . pray for him/her
Saint Peter and Saint Paul . . . . pray for him/her

Saint Andrew . . . . pray for him/her
Saint John. . . . . pray for him/her
Saint Mary Magdalene . . . . pray for him/her
Saint Stephen . . . . pray for him/her
Saint Ignatius . . . . pray for him/her
Saint Lawrence . . . . pray for him/her
Saint Perpetua and Saint Felicity. . . pray for him/her
Saint Agnes . . . . pray for him/her
Saint Gregory . . . . pray for him/her
Saint Augustine . . . . pray for him/her
Saint Athanasius. . . . . pray for him/her
Saint Basil . . . . pray for him/her
Saint Martin . . . . pray for him/her
Saint Benedict. . . . . pray for him/her
Saint Francis and Saint Dominic . . . pray for him/her
Saint Francis Xavier . . . . pray for him/her
Saint John Vianney . . . . pray for him/her
Saint Catherine. . . . . pray for him/her
Saint Teresa . . . . pray for him/her

Other saints may be included here.

All holy men and women . . . . pray for him/her

Lord, be merciful. . . . . Lord, save your people
From all evil . . . . Lord, save your people
From every sin . . . . Lord, save your people
From Satan's power . . . . Lord, save your people
At the moment of death. . . . . Lord, save your people
From everlasting death . . . . . Lord, save your people
On the day of judgment. . . . . Lord, save your people
By your coming as man . . . . Lord, save your people

By your suffering and cross. .   Lord, save your people
By your death
      and rising to new life . . Lord, save your people
By your return in glory
      to the Father . . . . Lord, save your people
By your gift
      of the Holy Spirit . . . . . Lord, save your people
By your coming again
      in glory . . . . Lord, save your people

Be merciful to us sinners. . . . . Lord, hear our prayer
Bring N. to eternal life,
      first promised to
      him/her in baptism. . . . Lord, hear our prayer
Raise N. on the last day,
      for he/she has eaten
      the bread of life . . . . . . Lord, hear our prayer
Let N. share in your glory,
      for he/she has shared in
      your suffering and death Lord, hear our prayer
Jesus, Son of the living God . . Lord, hear our prayer
Christ, hear us . . . . Christ, hear us
Lord Jesus, hear our prayer. . . Lord, hear our prayer

B

*A brief form of the litany may be prayed. Other saints may be added, including
the patron saints of the dying person, of the family, and of the parish; saints to
whom the dying person may have a special devotion may also be included.*

Holy Mary, Mother of God . . . . pray for him/her
Holy angels of God . . . . pray for him/her
Saint John the Baptist . . . . pray for him/her
Saint Joseph . . . . pray for him/her
Saint Peter and Saint Paul . . . . pray for him/her

Other saints may be included here.

All holy men and women . . . . pray for him/her

Prayer of Commendation

220   *When the moment of death seems near, some of the following prayers
may be said:*

A

Go forth, Christian soul, from this world
in the name of God the almighty Father,
who created you,
in the name of Jesus Christ, Son of the living God,
who suffered for you,
in the name of the Holy Spirit,
who was poured out upon you,
go forth, faithful Christian.

May you live in peace this day,
may your home be with God in Zion,
with Mary, the virgin Mother of God,
with Joseph, and all the angels and saints.

B

I commend you, my dear brother/sister,
to almighty God,
and entrust you to your Creator.
May you return to him
who formed you from the dust of the earth.
May holy Mary, the angels, and all the saints
come to meet you as you go forth from this life.
May Christ who was crucified for you
bring you freedom and peace.
May Christ who died for you
admit you into his garden of paradise.
May Christ, the true Shepherd,
acknowledge you as one of his flock.
May he forgive all your sins,
and set you among those he has chosen.
May you see your Redeemer face to face,
and enjoy the vision of God for ever.
R. Amen.

C

Welcome your servant, Lord, into the place of
salvation which because of your mercy he/she
rightly hoped for.
R. Amen, or *R. Lord, save your people.*

Deliver your servant, Lord, from every distress.
R. Amen, or *R. Lord, save your people.*

Deliver your servant, Lord, as you delivered Noah
from the flood.
R. *Amen,* or R. *Lord, save your people.*

Deliver your servant, Lord, as you delivered Abraham
from Ur of the Chaldees.
R. *Amen,* or R. *Lord, save your people.*

Deliver your servant, Lord, as you delivered Moses
from the hand of the Pharaoh.
R. *Amen,* or R. *Lord, save your people.*

Deliver your servant, Lord, as you delivered Daniel
from the den of lions.
R. *Amen,* or R. *Lord, save your people.*

Deliver your servant, Lord, as you delivered the three
young men from the fiery furnace.
R. *Amen,* or R. *Lord, save your people.*

Deliver your servant, Lord, as you delivered Susanna
from her false accusers.
R. *Amen,* or R. *Lord, save your people.*

Deliver your servant, Lord, as you delivered David
from the attacks of Saul and Goliath.
R. *Amen,* or R. *Lord, save your people.*

Deliver your servant, Lord, as you delivered Peter
and Paul from prison.
R. *Amen,* or R. *Lord, save your people.*

Deliver your servant, Lord, through Jesus our Savior,
who suffered death for us and gave us eternal life.
R. *Amen,* or R. *Lord, save your people.*

D

Lord Jesus Christ, Savior of the world,
we pray for your servant N.,
and commend him/her to your mercy.
For his/sake you came down from heaven;
receive him/her now into the joy of your kingdom.

For though he/she has sinned,
he she/has not denied the Father, the Son,
        and the Holy Spirit,
but has believed in God
and has worshipped his/her Creator.
R. *Amen.*

E   *The following antiphon may be said or sung:*

Hail, holy Queen, Mother of mercy,
hail, our life, our sweetness, and our hope.
To you we cry, the children of Eve;
to you we send up our sighs,
mourning and weeping in this land of exile.
Turn, then, most gracious advocate,
your eyes of mercy toward us;
lead us home at last

and show us the blessed fruit of your womb, Jesus:
O clement, O loving, O sweet Virgin Mary.

Prayer after Death

221 *When death has occurred, one or more of the following prayers may
be said:*

A

Saints of God, come to his/her aid!
Come to meet him/her, angels of the Lord!
R. *Receive his/her soul and present him/her to God the
Most High.*

May Christ, who called you, take you to himself; may
angels lead you to Abraham's side.
R. *Receive his/her soul and present him/her to God the
Most High.*

Give him/her eternal rest, O Lord,
and may your light shine on him/her for ever.
R. *Receive his/her soul and present him/her to God the
Most High.*

The following prayer is added:
Let us pray.

All-powerful and merciful God,
we commend to you N., your servant.

In your mercy and love,
blot out the sins he/she has committed
	through human weakness.
In this world he/she has died:
let him/her live with you for ever.

We ask this through Christ our Lord.
R. Amen.

*For the solace of those present the minister may conclude these prayers with
a simple blessing or with a symbolic gesture, for example, signing the forehead
with the sign of the cross.*

B PSALM 130

R. *My soul hopes in the Lord.*

Out of the depths I cry to you, O LORD;
	LORD, hear my voice!
Let your ears be attentive
	to my voice in supplication.
R. *My soul hopes in the Lord.*

I trust in the LORD,
	my soul trusts in his word.
My soul waits for the LORD
	more than sentinels wait for the dawn.
R. *My soul hopes in the Lord.*

For with the LORD is kindness,
	and with him is plenteous redemption.

And he will redeem Israel
     from all their iniquities.
R. *My soul hopes in the Lord.*

The following prayer is added:
Let us pray.
God of love, welcome into your presence
your son/daughter N., whom you have
     called from this life.
Release him/her from all his/her sins,
bless him/her with eternal light and peace,
raise him/her up to live for ever with all your saints
in the glory of the resurrection.

We ask this through Christ our Lord.
R. *Amen.*

C   PSALM 23

R. *Lord, remember me in your kingdom.*

The LORD is my shepherd; I shall not want.
     In verdant pastures he gives me repose;
Beside restful waters he leads me;
     he refreshes my soul.
R. *Lord, remember me in your kingdom.*

He guides me in right paths
     for his name's sake.

Even though I walk in the dark valley
     I fear no evil; for you are at my side
With your rod and your staff
     that give me courage.
R. *Lord, remember me in your kingdom.*

You spread the table before me
     in the sight of my foes;
You anoint my head with oil;
     my cup overflows.
R. *Lord, remember me in your kingdom.*

Only goodness and kindness follow me
     all the days of my life;
And I shall dwell in the house of the LORD
     for years to come.
R. *Lord, remember me in your kingdom.*

The following prayer is added:
Let us pray.
God of mercy,
hear our prayers and be merciful
to your son/daughter N.,
     whom you have called from this life.
Welcome him/her into the company of your saints,
in the kingdom of light and peace.

We ask this through Christ our Lord.
R. *Amen.*

D

Almighty and eternal God,
hear our prayers for your son/daughter N.,
whom you have called from this life to yourself.

Grant him/her light, happiness, and peace.
Let him/her pass in safety through the gates
of death,
and live for ever with all your saints
in the light you promised to Abraham
and to all his descendants in faith.

Guard him/her from all harm
and on that great day of resurrection and reward
raise him/her up with all your saints.
Pardon his/her sins
and give him/her eternal life in your kingdom.

We ask this through Christ our Lord.
R. Amen.

E

Loving and merciful God,
we entrust our brother/sister to your mercy.
You loved him/her greatly in this life:
now that he/she is freed from all its cares,
give him/her happiness and peace for ever.

The old order has passed away:
welcome him/her now into paradise

where there will be no more sorrow,
no more weeping or pain,
but only peace and joy
with Jesus, your Son,
and the Holy Spirit
for ever and ever.
R. Amen.

F

God of our destiny,
into your hands we commend our brother/sister.
We are confident that with all who have died in Christ
he/she will be raised to life on the last day
and live with Christ for ever.

[We thank you for all the blessings
you gave him/her in this life
to show your fatherly care for all of us
and the fellowship which is ours with the saints
        in Jesus Christ.]

Lord, hear our prayer:
welcome our brother/sister to paradise
and help us to comfort each other
with the assurance of our faith
until we all meet in Christ
to be with you and with our brother/sister for ever.

We ask this through Christ our Lord.
R. Amen.

Prayer for the Family and Friends

222   *The following prayer may be said:*

Let us pray.

A   *For the family and friends*

A God of all consolation,
in your unending love and mercy for us
you turn the darkness of death
into the dawn of new life.
Show compassion to your people in their sorrow.

[Be our refuge and our strength
to lift us from the darkness of this grief
to the peace and light of your presence.]

Your Son, our Lord Jesus Christ,
by dying for us, conquered death
and by rising again, restored life.

May we then go forward eagerly to meet him,
and after our life on earth
be reunited with our brothers and sisters
where every tear will be wiped away.
We ask this through Christ our Lord.
R. Amen.

B   *For the deceased person and for family and friends*

Lord Jesus, our Redeemer,
you willingly gave yourself up to death
so that all people might be saved

and pass from death into new life.
Listen to our prayers,
look with love on your people
who mourn and pray for their brother/sister N.

Lord Jesus, holy and compassionate:
forgive N. his/her sins.
By dying you opened the gates of life
for those who believe in you:
do not let our brother/sister be parted from you,
but by your glorious power
give him/her light, joy, and peace in heaven
where you live for ever and ever.
R. Amen.

*For the solace of those present the minister may conclude these prayers with
a simple blessing or with a symbolic gesture, for example, signing the forehead
with the sign of the cross.*

Prayers for the Dead

INTRODUCTION

I want those you have given me to be with me where I am.

223   This chapter contains prayers for use by a minister who has been called to attend a person who is already dead. A priest is not to administer the sacraments of penance or anointing. Instead, he should pray for the dead person using these or similar prayers.

224   It may be necessary to explain to the family of the person who is dead that sacraments are celebrated for the living, not for the dead, and that the dead are effectively helped by the prayers of the living.

225   To comfort those present the minister may conclude these prayers with a simple blessing or with a symbolic gesture, for example, making the sign of the cross on the forehead. A priest or deacon may sprinkle the body with holy water.

Greeting

226   *The minister greets those who are present, offering them sympathy and the consolation of faith, using the following or similar words:*

A
In this moment of sorrow
the Lord is in our midst
and comforts us with his word:
Blessed are the sorrowful; they shall be consoled.

B

Praised be God, the Father of our Lord Jesus Christ,
the Father of mercies,
and the God of all consolation!
He comforts us in all our afflictions
and thus enables us to comfort those who are
    in trouble,
with the same consolation
we have received from him.

Prayer

227   *The minister then says one of the following prayers, commending the*
person who has just died to God's mercy and goodness:

Let us pray.

A

Almighty and eternal God,
hear our prayers for your son/daughter N.,
whom you have called from this life to yourself.

Grant him/her light, happiness, and peace.
Let him/her pass in safety through the gates
    of death,
and live for ever with all your saints
in the light you promised to Abraham
and to all his descendants in faith.

Guard him/her from all harm
and on that great day of resurrection and reward
raise him/her up with all your saints.

Pardon his/her sins
and give him/her eternal life in your kingdom.

We ask this through Christ our Lord.
R. Amen.

B
Loving and merciful God,
we entrust our brother/sister to your mercy.
You loved him/her greatly in this life:
now that he/she is freed from all its cares,
give him/her happiness and peace for ever.

The old order has passed away:
welcome him/her now into paradise
where there will be no more sorrow,
no more weeping or pain,
but only peace and joy
with Jesus, your Son,
and the Holy Spirit
for ever and ever.
R. Amen.

Reading

228   *The word of God is proclaimed by one of those present or by the minister.*
One of the following readings may be used:

A Luke 23:44–46
B John 11:3–7, 20–27, 33–36, 41–44

Litany

Then one of those present may lead the others in praying a brief form of the litany of the saints. (The full form of the litany of the saints may be found in no. 219.) Other saints may be added, including the patron saints of the dead person, of the family, and of the parish; saints to whom the deceased person may have had a special devotion may also be included.

Saints of God, come to his/her aid!

Come to meet him/her, angels of the Lord!

Holy Mary, Mother of God	*pray for him/her*
Saint Joseph	*pray for him/her*
Saint Peter and Saint Paul	*pray for him/her*

The following prayer is added:

God of mercy,
hear our prayers and be merciful
to your son/daughter N., whom you have called
      from this life.
Welcome him/her into the company of your saints,
in the kingdom of light and peace.

We ask this through Christ our Lord.
R. *Amen.*

The Lord's Prayer

The minister introduces the Lord's Prayer in these or similar words:

A

With God there is mercy and fullness of redemption;
let us pray as Jesus taught us to pray:

B

Let us pray for the coming of the kingdom as Jesus taught us:

All say:

Our Father . . .

Prayer of Commendation

231   *The minister then concludes with the following prayer:*

Lord Jesus, our Redeemer,
you willingly gave yourself up to death
so that all people might be saved
and pass from death into a new life.
Listen to our prayers,
look with love on your people
who mourn and pray for their brother/sister N.

Lord Jesus, holy and compassionate:
forgive N. his/her sins.
By dying you opened the gates of life
for those who believe in you:
do not let our brother/sister be parted from you,
but by your glorious power
give him/her light, joy, and peace in heaven
where you live for ever and ever.
R. Amen.

*For the solace of those present the minister may conclude these prayers with
a simple blessing or with a symbolic gesture, for example, signing the forehead
with the sign of the cross.*

THE GOSPEL FOR SUNDAYS AND HOLY DAYS OF OBLIGATION

ADVENT

November 30, 2008

FIRST SUNDAY OF ADVENT

A reading from the holy Gospel according to Mark
13:33–37

Jesus said to his disciples:
"Be watchful! Be alert!
You do not know when the time will come.
It is like a man traveling abroad.
He leaves home and places his servants in charge,
  each with his own work,
  and orders the gatekeeper to be on the watch.
Watch, therefore;
  you do not know when the lord of the house
    is coming,
  whether in the evening, or at midnight,
  or at cockcrow, or in the morning.
May he not come suddenly and find you sleeping.
What I say to you, I say to all: 'Watch!'"

The Gospel of the Lord.

EXPLANATION OF THE READING

Through this holy season of Advent we look for the coming of the Lord.
We await his coming among us when we open the scriptures and

celebrate the sacraments. We look forward to the celebration of his birth in Bethlehem. Perhaps most importantly, though, we long and yearn for his coming again in glory at the end of time. Let us ask the Lord, then, to keep us always expectant of his coming, that he might not find us unaware.

December 7, 2008

SECOND SUNDAY OF ADVENT

A reading from the holy Gospel according to Mark
1:1–8

The beginning of the gospel of Jesus Christ
    the Son of God.

As it is written in Isaiah the prophet:
   Behold, I am sending my messenger ahead of you;
   he will prepare your way.
   A voice of one crying out in the desert:
    "Prepare the way of the Lord,
    make straight his paths."
John the Baptist appeared in the desert
   proclaiming a baptism of repentance for
     the forgiveness of sins.
People of the whole Judean countryside
   and all the inhabitants of Jerusalem
   were going out to him
   and were being baptized by him in the Jordan River
   as they acknowledged their sins.
John was clothed in camel's hair,
   with a leather belt around his waist.

He fed on locusts and wild honey.
And this is what he proclaimed:
   "One mightier than I is coming after me.
I am not worthy to stoop and loosen the thongs
      of his sandals.
I have baptized you with water;
   he will baptize you with the Holy Spirit."

The Gospel of the Lord.

EXPLANATION OF THE READING

The voice of John the Baptist filled the hearts of the people of Judah with
great joy because in his powerful words they heard the thundering voice
of truth. The forerunner of the Lord called the people to repentance so
that they might be inwardly prepared for the coming of the Messiah. Let
us listen intently to John's words and heed the humble sound of his voice
so that our hearts will exult when we hear at the last the majestic voice of
Christ Jesus.

December 8, 2008

SOLEMNITY OF THE IMMACULATE CONCEPTION OF THE BLESSED VIRGIN MARY

A reading from the holy Gospel according to Luke

1:26–38

The angel Gabriel was sent from God
   to a town of Galilee called Nazareth,
   to a virgin betrothed to a man named Joseph,
   of the house of David,
   and the virgin's name was Mary.

And coming to her, he said,
  "Hail, full of grace! The Lord is with you."
But she was greatly troubled at what was said
  and pondered what sort of greeting this might be.
Then the angel said to her,
  "Do not be afraid, Mary,
  for you have found favor with God.
Behold, you will conceive in your womb and bear
    a son,
  and you shall name him Jesus.
He will be great and will be called Son of
    the Most High,
  and the Lord God will give him the throne of
    David his father,
  and he will rule over the house of Jacob forever,
  and of his Kingdom there will be no end."
But Mary said to the angel,
  "How can this be,
  since I have no relations with a man?"
And the angel said to her in reply,
  "The Holy Spirit will come upon you,
  and the power of the Most High will
    overshadow you.
Therefore the child to be born
  will be called holy, the Son of God.
And behold, Elizabeth, your relative,
  has also conceived a son in her old age,

and this is the sixth month for her who was
  called barren;
for nothing will be impossible for God."
Mary said, "Behold, I am the handmaid of the Lord.
May it be done to me according to your word."
Then the angel departed from her.

The Gospel of the Lord.

EXPLANATION OF THE READING

Mary is for us the image of what we shall be if we remain faithful to the
call of the Lord Jesus. Conceived without sin, Mary received the life
intended for each of us. In this way she shows us the tender mercy and
love of the Father. He has not abandoned his children, but he lovingly
prepares the way for his Son, through Mary's cooperation, to destroy sin
and death and to take the throne of the house of David. Like Mary, let us
give ourselves completely to the Lord, withholding nothing from him.

December 14, 2008

THIRD SUNDAY OF ADVENT

A reading from the holy Gospel
according to John   *1:6–8, 19–28*

A man named John was sent from God.
He came for testimony, to testify to the light,
  so that all might believe through him.
He was not the light,
  but came to testify to the light.

And this is the testimony of John.
When the Jews from Jerusalem sent priests and
    Levites to him
  to ask him, "Who are you?"
  he admitted and did not deny it,
    but admitted, "I am not the Christ."
So they asked him,
    "What are you then? Are you Elijah?"
And he said, "I am not."
"Are you the Prophet?"
He answered, "No."
So they said to him,
    "Who are you, so we can give an answer
      to those who sent us?
What do you have to say for yourself?"
He said:
    "I am *the voice of one crying out in the desert,*
    'Make straight the way of the Lord,'
    as Isaiah the prophet said."
Some Pharisees were also sent.
They asked him,
    "Why then do you baptize
    if you are not the Christ or Elijah or the Prophet?"
John answered them,
    "I baptize with water;
    but there is one among you whom you
      do not recognize,
    the one who is coming after me,
    whose sandal strap I am not worthy to untie."

This happened in Bethany across the Jordan,
  where John was baptizing.

The Gospel of the Lord.

EXPLANATION OF THE READING

Today we pause in our joyful expectation of the Lord who has come, who is present, and who is to come. The announcement of the Baptist to "make straight the way of the Lord" is one taken from the heralds of the ancient kings. It was always a cry that entailed much toil as the people made everything proper for the monarch's visit, but one that also gave great joy, for it was not every day the king would come to town. Just as John's announcement gave joy to the people of old, so should it do for us. Our task is not the clearing of roads, but the clearing of the body, mind, and soul with repentance. Let us then make straight his way and look joyfully for his coming.

December 21, 2008

FOURTH SUNDAY OF ADVENT

A reading from the holy Gospel according to Luke
1:26–38

The angel Gabriel was sent from God
  to a town of Galilee called Nazareth,
  to a virgin betrothed to a man named Joseph,
  of the house of David,
  and the virgin's name was Mary.
And coming to her, he said,
  "Hail, full of grace! The Lord is with you."
But she was greatly troubled at what was said
  and pondered what sort of greeting this might be.

Then the angel said to her,
    "Do not be afraid, Mary,
    for you have found favor with God.

"Behold, you will conceive in your womb and
        bear a son,
    and you shall name him Jesus.
He will be great and will be called Son of
        the Most High,
    and the Lord God will give him the throne of
        David his father,
    and he will rule over the house of Jacob forever,
    and of his kingdom there will be no end."
But Mary said to the angel,
    "How can this be,
    since I have no relations with a man?"
And the angel said to her in reply,
    "The Holy Spirit will come upon you,
    and the power of the Most High will
        overshadow you.
Therefore the child to be born
    will be called holy, the Son of God.
    And behold, Elizabeth, your relative,
    has also conceived a son in her old age,
    and this is the sixth month for her who was
        called barren;
    for nothing will be impossible for God."
Mary said, "Behold, I am the handmaid of the Lord.

May it be done to me according to your word."
Then the angel departed from her.

The Gospel of the Lord.

EXPLANATION OF THE READING

The time is close at hand; our four weeks waiting in joyful hope are nearly fulfilled. As the days have passed, how well have we truly looked expectantly for the Lord? Have we allowed the joy of his love to well up within us? There still is time; it is not too late. The Light of the Nations is coming. Let us look to the east and watch him come to us.

CHRISTMAS

December 25, 2008

SOLEMNITY OF THE NATIVITY OF THE LORD

A reading from the holy Gospel according to Luke

2:1–14

In those days a decree went out from Caesar Augustus
    that the whole world should be enrolled.
This was the first enrollment,
    when Quirinius was governor of Syria.
So all went to be enrolled, each to his own town.
And Joseph too went up from Galilee from the town
        of Nazareth
    to Judea, to the city of David that is called Bethlehem,
    because he was of the house and family of David,
    to be enrolled with Mary, his betrothed,
        who was with child.
While they were there,
    the time came for her to have her child,
    and she gave birth to her firstborn son.
She wrapped him in swaddling clothes and laid him
        in a manger,
    because there was no room for them in the inn.

Now there were shepherds in that region living
    in the fields
  and keeping the night watch over their flock.
The angel of the Lord appeared to them
  and the glory of the Lord shone around them,
  and they were struck with great fear.
The angel said to them,
  "Do not be afraid;
  for behold, I proclaim to you good news of great joy
  that will be for all the people.
For today in the city of David
  a savior has been born for you who is Christ
    and Lord.
And this will be a sign for you:
  you will find an infant wrapped in swaddling clothes
  and lying in a manger."
And suddenly there was a multitude of
    the heavenly host with the angel,
  praising God and saying:
  "Glory to God in the highest
    and on earth peace to those on whom
      his favor rests."

The Gospel of the Lord.

EXPLANATION OF THE READING

Night's silence is broken by the wailing of the Word made flesh. Can this
be glory, this tiny child? We who have learned to see God's glory in the
otherness of God must now find it in a human child, who will grow into
a man and die, just as we all die. The creator has become a creature;
the infinite has become finite. God now speaks our language, too familiarly.
Incarnation commits us to full humanity for all people.

December 28, 2008

Feast of the Holy Family of Jesus, Mary, and Joseph

A reading from the holy Gospel according to Luke
2:22, 39-40

When the days were completed for their purification
   according to the law of Moses,
      they took him up to Jerusalem
      to present him to the Lord.

When they had fulfilled all the prescriptions
   of the law of the Lord,
      they returned to Galilee,
      to their own town of Nazareth.
The child grew and became strong, filled with wisdom;
   and the favor of God was upon him.

The Gospel of the Lord.

Longer form: Luke 2:22-40

EXPLANATION OF THE READING

On the feast of the Holy Family of Jesus, Mary, and Joseph, the Gospel
portrays Jesus opting for something more important than blood ties:
being in his Father's house. One senses a later Gospel scene and Jesus'
description of family: "my mother and my brothers are those who hear
the word of God and do it" (Luke 8:21). We who are "born not by natural
generation . . . but of God" (John 1:13) are called to live a new and radical
family life.

January 1, 2009

Solemnity of the Blessed Virgin Mary, Mother of God

A reading from the holy Gospel according to Luke

2:16–21

The shepherds went in haste to Bethlehem
    and found Mary and Joseph,
  and the infant lying in the manger.
When they saw this,
  they made known the message
  that had been told them about this child.
All who heard it were amazed
  by what had been told them by the shepherds.
And Mary kept all these things,
  reflecting on them in her heart.
Then the shepherds returned,
  glorifying and praising God
  for all they had heard and seen,
  just as it had been told to them.

When eight days were completed for his circumcision,
  he was named Jesus, the name given him
    by the angel
  before he was conceived in the womb.

The Gospel of the Lord.

EXPLANATION OF THE READING

Mary is the perfect example of a disciple of Christ Jesus, for she "kept all these things, reflecting on them in her heart." Never did the mysteries of Christ leave her thoughts or her prayers, and for this reason she followed him so faithfully. We often think, "Of course Mary pondered all these things, her encounter with God was so profound." This is indeed true, but is not our encounter with the Lord each day in the sacraments so very profound as well? Each day he comes to us, each day we experience his Passion, death, and Resurrection. Let us, with his Mother, keep these things in our heart. Let them never leave our minds and we, too, will follow faithfully after her Son.

January 4, 2009

SOLEMNITY OF THE EPIPHANY OF THE LORD

A reading from the holy Gospel according to Matthew
2:1–12

When Jesus was born in Bethlehem of Judea,
   in the days of King Herod,
   behold, magi from the east arrived in Jerusalem,
      saying,
   "Where is the newborn king of the Jews?
We saw his star at its rising
   and have come to do him homage."
When King Herod heard this,
   he was greatly troubled,
   and all Jerusalem with him.
Assembling all the chief priests and the scribes
      of the people,
   he inquired of them where the Christ was to be born.

They said to him, "In Bethlehem of Judea,
  for thus it has been written through the prophet:
    And you, Bethlehem, land of Judah,
      are by no means least among the rulers of Judah;
      since from you shall come a ruler,
        who is to shepherd my people Israel."
Then Herod called the magi secretly
  and ascertained from them the time of
    the star's appearance.
He sent them to Bethlehem and said,
  "Go and search diligently for the child.
When you have found him, bring me word,
  that I too may go and do him homage."
After their audience with the king they set out.
And behold, the star that they had seen at its rising
    preceded them,
  until it came and stopped over the place where
    the child was.
They were overjoyed at seeing the star,
  and on entering the house
    they saw the child with Mary his mother.
They prostrated themselves and did him homage.
Then they opened their treasures
  and offered him gifts of gold, frankincense,
    and myrrh.
And having been warned in a dream not to return
    to Herod,
  they departed for their country by another way.

The Gospel of the Lord.

EXPLANATION OF THE READING

After experiencing the love of Christ Jesus, the Magi would never be the same again—they were radically changed! This is why they "departed for their country by another way." As we have celebrated the birth of the Savior and have come to meet him in Bethlehem, have we allowed our encounter with him to change us? Have we allowed the power of his love to transform us and conform us ever more closely to his heart? May his love conquer our hearts and change us forever.

January 11, 2009

FEAST OF THE BAPTISM OF THE LORD

A reading from the holy Gospel according to Mark

1:7–11

This is what John the Baptist proclaimed:
  "One mightier than I is coming after me.
I am not worthy to stoop and loosen the thongs
    of his sandals.
I have baptized you with water;
  he will baptize you with the Holy Spirit."

It happened in those days that Jesus came from
    Nazareth of Galilee
  and was baptized in the Jordan by John.
On coming up out of the water he saw the heavens
    being torn open
  and the Spirit, like a dove, descending upon him.

And a voice came from the heavens,
  "You are my beloved Son; with you I am
    well pleased."

The Gospel of the Lord.

EXPLANATION OF THE READING

How worthy must one be to loosen someone's sandals? This is a task for
the lowest of servants, yet even so, John does not consider himself worthy
to remove Jesus' sandals. Such humility! John recognizes his unworthi-
ness to stand before the Son of God, and he readily and publicly admits it.
Too often do we pretend to be worthy of God, to be worthy of being his
servant. Through the gift of Baptism, not only does the Lord make us
worthy of his service, but he says to us, "With you I am well pleased." Let
us, then, serve the Lord and our brothers and sisters with joy and humility,
cognizant of the great gift with which he has lavished us.

Ordinary Time I

January 18, 2009

Second Sunday in Ordinary Time

A reading from the holy Gospel according to John
1:35–42

John was standing with two of his disciples,
   and as he watched Jesus walk by, he said,
   "Behold, the Lamb of God."
The two disciples heard what he said and
      followed Jesus.
Jesus turned and saw them following him and said
      to them,
   "What are you looking for?"
They said to him, "Rabbi"—which translated
      means Teacher—,
   "where are you staying?"
He said to them, "Come, and you will see."
So they went and saw where Jesus was staying,
   and they stayed with him that day.
It was about four in the afternoon.
Andrew, the brother of Simon Peter,
   was one of the two who heard John and
      followed Jesus.

He first found his own brother Simon and told him,
   "We have found the Messiah"—which is
      translated Christ—.
Then he brought him to Jesus.
Jesus looked at him and said,
   "You are Simon the son of John;
   you will be called Cephas"—which is
      translated Peter.

The Gospel of the Lord.

EXPLANATION OF THE READING

Have you ever heard the saying, "It's not all about you!" or the old Zen quote, "A finger pointing to the moon is not the moon"? Wisely, John the Baptist realized that he was not "the moon." In the passage preceding today's Gospel, John tells people he is not the Messiah, and seeing Jesus, he exclaimed, "Behold the Lamb of God." In today's Gospel, he points to Jesus again. John's disciples then followed Jesus. Who points you to Jesus?

January 25, 2009

THIRD SUNDAY IN ORDINARY TIME

A reading from the holy Gospel according to Mark
1:14–20

After John had been arrested,
   Jesus came to Galilee proclaiming the gospel of God:
   "This is the time of fulfillment.
The kingdom of God is at hand.
Repent, and believe in the gospel."

As he passed by the Sea of Galilee,
  he saw Simon and his brother Andrew casting
    their nets into the sea;
  they were fishermen.
Jesus said to them,
  "Come after me, and I will make you fishers of men."
Then they abandoned their nets and followed him.
He walked along a little farther
  and saw James, the son of Zebedee,
    and his brother John.
They too were in a boat mending their nets.
Then he called them.
So they left their father Zebedee in the boat
  along with the hired men and followed him.

The Gospel of the Lord.

EXPLANATION OF THE READING

A fisherman's life is constant and grueling, at sea and on land. There are always nets to tend or boats to repair. In many professions today, 60-hour-plus work weeks are the norm. We never seem to get caught up. Peter, James, and John worked hard, but they were still open to following Jesus. It is interesting that Jesus came to them in the workplace. How does Christ meet you in your job? How do you follow Jesus?

FOURTH SUNDAY IN ORDINARY TIME

A reading from the holy Gospel according to Mark
1:21–28

Then they came to Capernaum,
  and on the sabbath Jesus entered the synagogue
    and taught.
The people were astonished at his teaching,
  for he taught them as one having authority and
    not as the scribes.
In their synagogue was a man with an unclean spirit;
  he cried out, "What have you to do with us,
    Jesus of Nazareth?
Have you come to destroy us?
I know who you are—the Holy One of God!"
Jesus rebuked him and said,
  "Quiet! Come out of him!"
The unclean spirit convulsed him and with a loud cry
    came out of him.
All were amazed and asked one another,
  "What is this?
A new teaching with authority.
He commands even the unclean spirits and
    they obey him."
His fame spread everywhere throughout
    the whole region of Galilee.

The Gospel of the Lord.

EXPLANATION OF THE READING

Did you ever hear a homilist who was smart but dry as a bone? Now contrast that with an energetic speaker who makes eye contact and has great vocal inflections. The people may have been surprised, but Jesus definitely caught and held their attention. It is interesting that evil recognized his authority before goodness. Are we open to Jesus working in our lives, or do we resist and question his teachings? We must choose Christ.

February 8, 2009

FIFTH SUNDAY IN ORDINARY TIME

A reading from the holy Gospel according to Mark
1:29–39

On leaving the synagogue
    Jesus entered the house of Simon and Andrew
        with James and John.
Simon's mother-in-law lay sick with a fever.
They immediately told him about her.
He approached, grasped her hand, and helped her up.
Then the fever left her and she waited on them.

When it was evening, after sunset,
    they brought to him all who were ill or
        possessed by demons.
The whole town was gathered at the door.
He cured many who were sick with various diseases,
    and he drove out many demons,
        not permitting them to speak because
            they knew him.

Rising very early before dawn, he left
 and went off to a deserted place, where he prayed.
Simon and those who were with him pursued him
 and on finding him said, "Everyone is looking
  for you."
He told them, "Let us go on to the nearby villages
 that I may preach there also.
For this purpose have I come."
So he went into their synagogues,
 preaching and driving out demons throughout
  the whole of Galilee.

The Gospel of the Lord.

EXPLANATION OF THE READING

The Benedictine model *ora et labora*, "work and pray," applies to today's
Gospel. Jesus is never either/or, but he is both/and. We think, "Oh, I am so
busy with my (fill in your blank); there will be time to pray later." Life and
experience prove otherwise. Give God the freshest part of your day. It is
like the saving concept of paying yourself first before the bills. If we do not
consciously do it, it will not happen. Pray.

February 15, 2009

SIXTH SUNDAY IN ORDINARY TIME

A reading from the holy Gospel
according to Mark   1:40–45

A leper came to Jesus and kneeling down begged him
 and said,
 "If you wish, you can make me clean."

Moved with pity, he stretched out his hand,
   touched him, and said to him,
   "I do will it. Be made clean."
The leprosy left him immediately,
   and he was made clean.
Then, warning him sternly, he dismissed him at once.

He said to him, "See that you tell no one anything,
   but go, show yourself to the priest
   and offer for your cleansing what Moses prescribed;
   that will be proof for them."

The man went away and began to publicize
   the whole matter.
He spread the report abroad
   so that it was impossible for Jesus to enter
   a town openly.
He remained outside in deserted places,
   and people kept coming to him from everywhere.

The Gospel of the Lord.

EXPLANATION OF THE READING

In today's world, we are often taught about self-esteem and pride, but not very much about humility. In fact, we have become used to having our own way. The leper is in a very vulnerable position as he approaches Jesus and kneels before him. How hard it must have been to ask for help, and to risk possible rejection. Keep that in mind the next time someone less fortunate than you asks for your help, and follow Christ's example.

February 22, 2009

SEVENTH SUNDAY IN ORDINARY TIME

A reading from the holy Gospel according to Mark
2:1–12

When Jesus returned to Capernaum after some days,
  it became known that he was at home.
Many gathered together so that there was no longer
    room for them,
  not even around the door,
  and he preached the word to them.
They came bringing to him a paralytic carried by
    four men.
Unable to get near Jesus because of the crowd,
  they opened up the roof above him.
After they had broken through,
  they let down the mat on which the paralytic
    was lying.
When Jesus saw their faith, he said to the paralytic,
  "Child, your sins are forgiven."
Now some of the scribes were sitting there
    asking themselves,
  "Why does this man speak that way?
  He is blaspheming.
Who but God alone can forgive sins?"
Jesus immediately knew in his mind
  what they were thinking to themselves,
  so he said, "Why are you thinking such things
    in your hearts?

Which is easier, to say to the paralytic,
   'Your sins are forgiven,'
   or to say, 'Rise, pick up your mat and walk'?
But that you may know
   that the Son of Man has authority to forgive sins
      on earth"
   —he said to the paralytic,
   "I say to you, rise, pick up your mat, and go home."
He rose, picked up his mat at once,
   and went away in the sight of everyone.
They were all astounded
   and glorified God, saying, "We have never seen
      anything like this."

The Gospel of the Lord.

EXPLANATION OF THE READING

We see Jesus as healer again, only this time he does something even greater than physical healing. Jesus is in Capernaum again, where he cast out the demon from a man in the synagogue. Word has spread, and the house is so crowded with people that it is impossible to get in at the door. Undaunted, four friends lower their paralyzed friend through the roof of the house. Jesus, seeing their faith, speaks to the paralyzed man tenderly: "Child, your sins are forgiven" (Mark 2:5). The people are shocked, and the scribes are indignant. They do not speak aloud, but whisper among themselves: Who is this man to be forgiving sins? Only God can forgive! Jesus then proves his authority by speaking again to the paralyzed man, this time with words of healing—and the paralyzed man gets up and goes out, freed of his burdens, both mental and physical. As with all the wonders Jesus works, the healing of the paralytic is not an end in itself, but a sign that demonstrates Jesus' authority to forgive and leads others to faith. For all present were "astounded and glorified God" (Mark 2:12) at the new thing that had happened in their midst. Isaiah's prophecy is being fulfilled, for those with the eyes to see it.

LENT

March 1, 2009

FIRST SUNDAY OF LENT

A reading from the holy Gospel according to Mark

1:12–15

The Spirit drove Jesus out into the desert,
  and he remained in the desert for forty days,
    tempted by Satan.
He was among wild beasts,
  and the angels ministered to him.

After John had been arrested,
  Jesus came to Galilee proclaiming the gospel of God:
  "This is the time of fulfillment.
The kingdom of God is at hand.
Repent, and believe in the gospel."

The Gospel of the Lord.

EXPLANATION OF THE READING

Through the generosity of the most merciful Lord, the time of fulfillment is always at hand; every time is ripe for repentance and reconciliation. For what, then, are we waiting? Today thousands of men and women the world over will stand before their bishops and be numbered among the elect while others are called to continuing conversion. Let the example of these souls who long for God's love inspire us to a more faithful following of the Lord Jesus Christ. Let us, with them, repent of our sins and seek his tender mercy that long life and contentment will be ours.

March 8, 2009

SECOND SUNDAY OF LENT

A reading from the holy Gospel according to Mark   *9:2–10*

Jesus took Peter, James, and John
  and led them up a high mountain apart
    by themselves.
And he was transfigured before them,
  and his clothes became dazzling white,
  such as no fuller on earth could bleach them.
Then Elijah appeared to them along with Moses,
  and they were conversing with Jesus.
Then Peter said to Jesus in reply,
  "Rabbi, it is good that we are here!
Let us make three tents:
  one for you, one for Moses, and one for Elijah."
He hardly knew what to say, they were so terrified.
Then a cloud came, casting a shadow over them;
  from the cloud came a voice,
  "This is my beloved Son. Listen to him."
Suddenly, looking around, they no longer saw anyone
  but Jesus alone with them.

As they were coming down from the mountain,
   he charged them not to relate what they had
     seen to anyone,
   except when the Son of Man had risen from the dead.
So they kept the matter to themselves,
   questioning what rising from the dead meant.

The Gospel of the Lord.

EXPLANATION OF THE READING

Although we have been journeying through Lent for only one week now, many of us have already grown weary of this way and have fallen asleep. Some are weary from genuine penitential practices and need a glimpse of the Lord's glory to see the end goal. Some are weary of their sins and need to see the glory of the Lord that is his love. Others, yet, need to see the Lord transfigured to wake them from their slumber, induced by indifference. Let us not fall spiritually asleep. Rather, let us remain attentive to the one who fulfills the law and the prophets.

March 15, 2009

THIRD SUNDAY OF LENT

A reading from the holy Gospel according to John
2:13–25

Since the Passover of the Jews was near,
   Jesus went up to Jerusalem.
He found in the temple area those who sold oxen,
   sheep, and doves,
   as well as the money changers seated there.

He made a whip out of cords
and drove them all out of the temple area,
with the sheep and oxen,
and spilled the coins of the money changers
and overturned their tables,
and to those who sold doves he said,
"Take these out of here,
and stop making my Father's house a marketplace."
His disciples recalled the words of Scripture,
Zeal for your house will consume me.
At this the Jews answered and said to him,
"What sign can you show us for doing this?"
Jesus answered and said to them,
"Destroy this temple and in three days
I will raise it up."
The Jews said,
"This temple has been under construction
for forty-six years,
and you will raise it up in three days?"
But he was speaking about the temple of his body.
Therefore, when he was raised from the dead,
his disciples remembered that he had said this,
and they came to believe the Scripture
and the word Jesus had spoken.

While he was in Jerusalem for the feast of Passover,
many began to believe in his name
when they saw the signs he was doing.

But Jesus would not trust himself to them because
    he knew them all,
  and did not need anyone to testify
    about human nature.
He himself understood it well.

The Gospel of the Lord.

EXPLANATION OF THE READING

We often convince ourselves that the Lord will not understand our
situations and circumstances, and therefore will not understand our
thoughts and our actions. It seems that he expects too much of us
sinners—that we cannot measure up to his high calling. In these times we
would do well to remember the last lines of the Gospel. Jesus understands
our human nature so well that he understands both our sinfulness and our
failings. Even so, he desires us to live in his house.

March 22, 2009

FOURTH SUNDAY OF LENT

A reading from the holy Gospel according to John

3:14–21

Jesus said to Nicodemus:
  "Just as Moses lifted up the serpent in the desert,
  so must the Son of Man be lifted up,
  so that everyone who believes in him may have
    eternal life."

For God so loved the world that he gave his only Son,
    so that everyone who believes in him
        might not perish
    but might have eternal life.
For God did not send his Son into the world
    to condemn the world,
    but that the world might be saved through him.
Whoever believes in him will not be condemned,
    but whoever does not believe has already
        been condemned,
    because he has not believed in the name of
        the only Son of God.
And this is the verdict,
    that the light came into the world,
    but people preferred darkness to light,
    because their works were evil.
For everyone who does wicked things hates the light
    and does not come toward the light,
    so that his works might not be exposed.
But whoever lives the truth comes to the light,
    so that his works may be clearly seen as done
        in God.

The Gospel of the Lord.

EXPLANATION OF THE READING

Today the liturgy calls us to refocus our attention from the magnitude of sins to the unfathomable mercies of God. Holy Mother Church invites her children to rejoice in the merciful love of the Father that we will experience in two weeks' time as we experience Good Friday. Lent is a joyful season, because even as we come to a more profound awareness of sin, we come to a deeper experience and appreciation of the Lord's mercy. What greater joy can there be than this!

March 29, 2009

FIFTH SUNDAY OF LENT

A reading from the holy Gospel according to John

12:20–33

Some Greeks who had come to worship at
    the Passover Feast
  came to Philip, who was from Bethsaida in Galilee,
  and asked him, "Sir, we would like to see Jesus."
Philip went and told Andrew;
  then Andrew and Philip went and told Jesus.
Jesus answered them,
  "The hour has come for the Son of Man
    to be glorified.
Amen, amen, I say to you,
  unless a grain of wheat falls to the ground and dies,
  it remains just a grain of wheat;
  but if it dies, it produces much fruit.
Whoever loves his life loses it,
  and whoever hates his life in this world
  will preserve it for eternal life.
Whoever serves me must follow me,
  and where I am, there also will my servant be.
The Father will honor whoever serves me.

"I am troubled now. Yet what should I say,
'Father, save me from this hour'?
But it was for this purpose that I came to this hour.
Father, glorify your name."
Then a voice came from heaven,
  "I have glorified it and will glorify it again."
The crowd there heard it and said it was thunder;
  but others said, "An angel has spoken to him."
Jesus answered and said,
  "This voice did not come for my sake but for yours.
Now is the time of judgment on this world;
  now the ruler of this world will be driven out.
And when I am lifted up from the earth,
  I will draw everyone to myself."
He said this indicating the kind of death he would die.

The Gospel of the Lord.

EXPLANATION OF THE READING

Jesus is clear in saying that if we desire to look upon his splendor, we
must die to ourselves and so live in him. We must set aside our own proud
ambitions and desires. We must seek to follow the will of Christ by
imitating the model he has given us, that of self-emptying love. When we
hand over our lives to Jesus, the Father will glorify his name as we become
one with Jesus. Let us then seek not to avoid the pain of penance and
conversion, but let us rather embrace this pain and, like the grain of
wheat, die to our sinful desires.

April 5, 2009

Palm Sunday of the Lord's Passion

The Passion of our Lord Jesus Christ according to Mark

15:1–39

As soon as morning came,
  the chief priests with the elders and the scribes,
  that is, the whole Sanhedrin, held a council.
They bound Jesus, led him away, and handed him
      over to Pilate.
Pilate questioned him,
  "Are you the king of the Jews?"
He said to him in reply, "You say so."
The chief priests accused him of many things.
Again Pilate questioned him,
  "Have you no answer?
See how many things they accuse you of."
Jesus gave him no further answer, so that Pilate
      was amazed.

Now on the occasion of the feast he used to release
      to them
  one prisoner whom they requested.
A man called Barabbas was then in prison
  along with the rebels who had committed murder
      in a rebellion.
The crowd came forward and began to ask him
  to do for them as he was accustomed.

Pilate answered,
   "Do you want me to release to you the king of
      the Jews?"
For he knew that it was out of envy
   that the chief priests had handed him over.
But the chief priests stirred up the crowd
   to have him release Barabbas for them instead.
Pilate again said to them in reply,
   "Then what do you want me to do
   with the man you call the king of the Jews?"
They shouted again, "Crucify him."
Pilate said to them, "Why? What evil has he done?"
They only shouted the louder, "Crucify him."
So Pilate, wishing to satisfy the crowd,
   released Barabbas to them and,
      after he had Jesus scourged,
   handed him over to be crucified.

The soldiers led him away inside the palace,
   that is, the praetorium, and assembled
      the whole cohort.
They clothed him in purple and,
   weaving a crown of thorns, placed it on him.
They began to salute him with,
      "Hail, King of the Jews!"
   and kept striking his head with a reed and
      spitting upon him.
They knelt before him in homage.

And when they had mocked him,
　　they stripped him of the purple cloak,
　　dressed him in his own clothes,
　　and led him out to crucify him.

They pressed into service a passer-by, Simon,
　　a Cyrenian, who was coming in from the country,
　　the father of Alexander and Rufus,
　　to carry his cross.

They brought him to the place of Golgotha
　　—which is translated Place of the Skull—.
They gave him wine drugged with myrrh,
　　but he did not take it.
Then they crucified him and divided his garments
　　by casting lots for them to see what each
　　　　should take.
It was nine o'clock in the morning when
　　　　they crucified him.
The inscription of the charge against him read,
　　"The King of the Jews."
With him they crucified two revolutionaries,
　　one on his right and one on his left.
Those passing by reviled him,
　　shaking their heads and saying,
　　"Aha! You who would destroy the temple
　　and rebuild it in three days,
　　save yourself by coming down from the cross."

Likewise the chief priests, with the scribes,
   mocked him among themselves and said,
   "He saved others; he cannot save himself.
Let the Christ, the King of Israel,
   come down now from the cross
   that we may see and believe."
Those who were crucified with him also kept
      abusing him.

At noon darkness came over the whole land
   until three in the afternoon.
And at three o'clock Jesus cried out in a loud voice,
   "Eloi, Eloi, lema sabachthani?"
   which is translated,
   "My God, my God, why have you forsaken me?"
Some of the bystanders who heard it said,
   "Look, he is calling Elijah."
One of them ran, soaked a sponge with wine,
      put it on a reed
   and gave it to him to drink saying,
   "Wait, let us see if Elijah comes to take him down."
Jesus gave a loud cry and breathed his last.

[Here all kneel and pause for a short time.]

The veil of the sanctuary was torn in two from
      top to bottom.

When the centurion who stood facing him
saw how he breathed his last he said,
"Truly this man was the Son of God!"

The Gospel of the Lord.

Longer form: Mark 14:1–15:47

EXPLANATION OF THE READING

Mark's account of the Crucifixion may be the shortest of the four, but it is perhaps the most dramatic. After Jesus "breathed his last" (Mark 15:37), everything changes. The veil of the sanctuary is torn, and the Roman centurion proclaims Jesus "the Son of God" (Mark 15:39). Suddenly we discover that Jesus was not totally abandoned, since "women looking on from a distance" (Mark 15:40) now come forward, as does Joseph of Arimathea, who fearlessly asks for the body of Jesus. Christ's death on the cross has already begun its work of transformation. At the beginning of the Passion, a community was scattered. At the end, a new community is beginning to gather around the body of Jesus, to await the Resurrection.

EASTER

April 12, 2009

EASTER SUNDAY: SOLEMNITY OF THE RESURRECTION OF THE LORD

A reading from the holy Gospel according to John

20:1–9

On the first day of the week,
  Mary of Magdala came to the tomb early
    in the morning,
  while it was still dark,
  and saw the stone removed from the tomb.
So she ran and went to Simon Peter
  and to the other disciple whom Jesus loved,
    and told them,
  "They have taken the Lord from the tomb,
  and we don't know where they put him."
So Peter and the other disciple went out and came
    to the tomb.
They both ran, but the other disciple ran faster
    than Peter
  and arrived at the tomb first;
  he bent down and saw the burial cloths there,
    but did not go in.

Simon Peter arrived after him,
    went into the tomb and saw
    the burial cloths there,
and the cloth that had covered his head,
not with the burial cloths but rolled up
    in a separate place.
Then the other disciple also went in,
    the one who had arrived at the tomb first,
    and he saw and believed.
For they did not yet understand the Scripture
    that he had to rise from the dead.

The Gospel of the Lord.

EXPLANATION OF THE READING

Mary of Magdala arrives at the tomb while it is still dark; in her love for
Jesus, she cannot stay away. She is compelled to come and look for him.
Peter and John's curiosity and love compel them to hasten to the tomb.
They, too, cannot stay away. Such should be our attitude today. The news
of the Resurrection should enliven within us a great love of the Lord,
prompting us to hasten our journey to the kingdom, all the while
proclaiming the greatness of his love.

April 19, 2009

SECOND SUNDAY OF EASTER/ DIVINE MERCY SUNDAY

A reading from the holy Gospel according to John

20:19–31

On the evening of that first day of the week,
   when the doors were locked,
      where the disciples were,
   for fear of the Jews,
   Jesus came and stood in their midst
   and said to them, "Peace be with you."
When he had said this, he showed them his hands
      and his side.
The disciples rejoiced when they saw the Lord.
Jesus said to them again, "Peace be with you.
As the Father has sent me, so I send you."
And when he had said this, he breathed on them
      and said to them,
   "Receive the Holy Spirit.
Whose sins you forgive are forgiven them,
   and whose sins you retain are retained."

Thomas, called Didymus, one of the Twelve,
   was not with them when Jesus came.
So the other disciples said to him,
      "We have seen the Lord."
But he said to them,
   "Unless I see the mark of the nails in his hands

and put my finger into the nailmarks
and put my hand into his side, I will not believe."

Now a week later his disciples were again inside
and Thomas was with them.
Jesus came, although the doors were locked,
and stood in their midst and said,
"Peace be with you."
Then he said to Thomas,
"Put your finger here and see my hands,
and bring your hand and put it into my side,
and do not be unbelieving, but believe."
Thomas answered and said to him,
"My Lord and my God!"
Jesus said to him, "Have you come to believe
because you have seen me?
Blessed are those who have not seen and
have believed."

Now Jesus did many other signs in the presence
of his disciples
that are not written in this book.
But these are written that you may come to believe
that Jesus is the Christ, the Son of God,
and that through this belief you may have life
in his name.

The Gospel of the Lord.

EXPLANATION OF THE READING

If Jesus were to stand before us and we were to behold him with our eyes, what would we expect him to say? Our minds would probably be flooded with many thoughts and questions we would like him to address. Yet he would say only, "Peace be with you." It is through the gift of his great mercy that our hearts are calmed and we find peace. In such peace, we have no more need of physical reassurances of the Resurrection.

April 26, 2009

THIRD SUNDAY OF EASTER

A reading from the holy Gospel according to Luke

24:35–48

The two disciples recounted what had taken place
    on the way,
    and how Jesus was made known to them
    in the breaking of bread.

While they were still speaking about this,
    he stood in their midst and said to them,
    "Peace be with you."
But they were startled and terrified
    and thought that they were seeing a ghost.
Then he said to them, "Why are you troubled?
And why do questions arise in your hearts?
Look at my hands and my feet, that it is I myself.
Touch me and see, because a ghost does not have
    flesh and bones
    as you can see I have."

And as he said this,
   he showed them his hands and his feet.
While they were still incredulous for joy and
     were amazed,
   he asked them, "Have you anything here to eat?"
They gave him a piece of baked fish;
   he took it and ate it in front of them.

He said to them,
   "These are my words that I spoke to you while
     I was still with you,
   that everything written about me in the law of Moses
   and in the prophets and psalms must be fulfilled."
Then he opened their minds to understand
     the Scriptures.
And he said to them,
   "Thus it is written that the Christ would suffer
   and rise from the dead on the third day
   and that repentance, for the forgiveness of sins,
   would be preached in his name
   to all the nations, beginning from Jerusalem.
You are witnesses of these things."

The Gospel of the Lord.

EXPLANATION OF THE READING

When we consider all that the Lord has done for our salvation, the
questions he poses today cut straight to the heart: "Why are you
troubled? And why do questions arise in your hearts?" If God himself
would suffer death for our sakes and rise from the dead, what have we to
fear? Will he not meet all of our needs if he has gone this far? Gazing upon

the wounds he bears and encountering him in the Eucharist, we must open ourselves to his gift of peace.

May 3, 2009

Fourth Sunday of Easter

A reading from the holy Gospel according to John

10:11–18

Jesus said:
"I am the good shepherd.
A good shepherd lays down his life for the sheep.
A hired man, who is not a shepherd
and whose sheep are not his own,
sees a wolf coming and leaves the sheep
and runs away,
and the wolf catches and scatters them.
This is because he works for pay and has no concern
for the sheep.
I am the good shepherd,
and I know mine and mine know me,
just as the Father knows me and I know the Father;
and I will lay down my life for the sheep.
I have other sheep that do not belong to this fold.
These also I must lead, and they will hear my voice,
and there will be one flock, one shepherd.
This is why the Father loves me,
because I lay down my life in order to take
it up again.

No one takes it from me, but I lay it down on my own.
I have power to lay it down, and power to take
    it up again.
This command I have received from my Father."

The Gospel of the Lord.

EXPLANATION OF THE READING

Jesus is the Good Shepherd; he knows his sheep and his sheep know him. In our times, following someone like a sheep follows a shepherd may not sound like something we want to do, but consider the intimacy of the relationship that Jesus describes in this passage. He knows his own like his Father knows him. Jesus and the Father are one, and he extends the intimacy of this relationship to us and to all of his sheep. Wherever his sheep graze, they will hear his voice.

May 10, 2009

FIFTH SUNDAY OF EASTER

A reading from the holy Gospel according to John
15:1–8

Jesus said to his disciples:
    "I am the true vine, and my Father is the vine grower.
He takes away every branch in me that does not
    bear fruit,
    and every one that does he prunes so that
    it bears more fruit.
You are already pruned because of the word that
    I spoke to you.
Remain in me, as I remain in you.

Just as a branch cannot bear fruit on its own
    unless it remains on the vine,
    so neither can you unless you remain in me.
I am the vine, you are the branches.
Whoever remains in me and I in him will bear
        much fruit,
    because without me you can do nothing.
Anyone who does not remain in me
    will be thrown out like a branch and wither;
    people will gather them and throw them into a fire
    and they will be burned.
If you remain in me and my words remain in you,
    ask for whatever you want and it will be done
        for you.
By this is my Father glorified,
    that you bear much fruit and become
        my disciples."

The Gospel of the Lord.

EXPLANATION OF THE READING

The Gospel is drawn from the Last Supper discourses, which follow the accounts of the washing of the feet and the betrayal by Judas in the Gospel according to John. *What does it mean to "remain" in Jesus (John 15:4)?* The metaphor of the vine and branches helps us to understand. The branches are absolutely dependent on the vine: if they are cut away, they wither at once. But the vine needs the branches as well, for the branches can bear fruit. The imagery of today's Gospel speaks of a great intimacy. We are like branches on the vine, intimately connected with our source of life, sharing one existence. "We cannot distinguish what is of God and what is of us".

May 17, 2009

Sixth Sunday of Easter

A reading from the holy Gospel according to John

15:9–17

Jesus said to his disciples:
"As the Father loves me, so I also love you.
Remain in my love.
If you keep my commandments, you will remain
     in my love,
  just as I have kept my Father's commandments
  and remain in his love.

"I have told you this so that my joy may be in you
  and your joy might be complete.
This is my commandment: love one another as
     I love you.
No one has greater love than this,
  to lay down one's life for one's friends.
You are my friends if you do what I command you.
I no longer call you slaves,
  because a slave does not know what his master
    is doing.
I have called you friends,
  because I have told you everything I have heard
    from my Father.
It was not you who chose me, but I who chose you
  and appointed you to go and bear fruit
    that will remain,

so that whatever you ask the Father in my name
   he may give you.
This I command you: love one another."

The Gospel of the Lord.

EXPLANATION OF THE READING

We are loved. We are chosen. We are friends of Christ. We should be joyful. So, why do so many of us complain about "having" to go to church? We gripe about following so many rules. We look around and judge the people in the pews. Jesus said, "Love one another." Take another look at the members of Body of Christ, the Church — we are loved, we are chosen, Christ calls us friends. Rejoice!

May 21, 2009 or May 24, 2009

SOLEMNITY OF THE ASCENSION OF THE LORD

A reading from the holy Gospel according to Mark
16:15 – 20

Jesus said to his disciples:
   "Go into the whole world
   and proclaim the gospel to every creature.
Whoever believes and is baptized will be saved;
   whoever does not believe will be condemned.
These signs will accompany those who believe:
   in my name they will drive out demons,
   they will speak new languages.

·

They will pick up serpents with their hands,
　　and if they drink any deadly thing,
　　　　it will not harm them.
They will lay hands on the sick, and they will recover."

So then the Lord Jesus, after he spoke to them,
　　was taken up into heaven
　　and took his seat at the right hand of God.
But they went forth and preached everywhere,
　　while the Lord worked with them
　　and confirmed the word through
　　　　accompanying signs.

The Gospel of the Lord.

EXPLANATION OF THE READING

In this Year B we hear the conclusion of the Gospel according to Mark, along with the great commission Christ gives his disciples. They are to go into the whole world, so that every creature on earth may hear the Good News. If they believe, amazing signs will accompany their preaching. At the end of the reading, Jesus is taken into heaven, and the disciples "went forth and preached everywhere" (Mark 16:20). However, the end of the reading makes clear that Jesus is not gone. Rather, he is even more with them than before: "the Lord worked with them and confirmed the word through accompanying signs" (Mark 16:20).

May 24, 2009

SEVENTH SUNDAY OF EASTER

A reading from the holy Gospel according to John

17:11b–19

Lifting up his eyes to heaven, Jesus prayed, saying:
 "Holy Father, keep them in your name that
  you have given me,
 so that they may be one just as we are one.
When I was with them I protected them in your name
  that you gave me,
 and I guarded them, and none of them was lost
 except the son of destruction,
 in order that the Scripture might be fulfilled.
But now I am coming to you.
I speak this in the world
 so that they may share my joy completely.
I gave them your word, and the world hated them,
 because they do not belong to the world
 any more than I belong to the world.
I do not ask that you take them out of the world
 but that you keep them from the evil one.
They do not belong to the world
 any more than I belong to the world.
Consecrate them in the truth. Your word is truth.
As you sent me into the world,
 so I sent them into the world.

And I consecrate myself for them,
   so that they also may be consecrated in truth."

The Gospel of the Lord.

EXPLANATION OF THE READING

The Gospel is drawn from what is called the "high priestly prayer" of Jesus at the conclusion of the Last Supper discourses in the Gospel according to John. Immediately before his arrest, Jesus prays for his disciples. He prays "that they may be one just as we are one" (John 17:11). He does not pray that their lives will be easy—indeed, it is clear that they will face the same trials Jesus himself faced. They will be hated by a world in which they cannot feel at home, for "they do not belong to the world any more than I belong to the world" (John 17:14). They are sent forth nevertheless, not only witnesses to Jesus, but sharers in his love, his joy, and his peace.

May 31, 2009

SOLEMNITY OF PENTECOST

A reading from the holy Gospel according to John

20:19–23

On the evening of that first day of the week,
   when the doors were locked,
      where the disciples were,
   for fear of the Jews,
   Jesus came and stood in their midst
   and said to them, "Peace be with you."
When he had said this, he showed them his hands
      and his side.
The disciples rejoiced when they saw the Lord.
Jesus said to them again, "Peace be with you.

As the Father has sent me, so I send you."
And when he had said this, he breathed on them
    and said to them,
  "Receive the Holy Spirit.
Whose sins you forgive are forgiven them,
    and whose sins you retain are retained."

The Gospel of the Lord.

EXPLANATION OF THE READING

In this Year B we have read from the Gospel according to John throughout
the Easter season. In today's reading from the Last Supper discourses,
Jesus tells his disciples about the Spirit. The Holy Spirit will be their
"Advocate" (John 15:26). The Holy Spirit will also be teacher and guide,
telling them "the things that are coming" (John 16:13). The Holy Spirit will
be God's very presence among them, for the Holy Spirit "proceeds from
the Father" (John 15:26). The Holy Spirit is the gift of a recklessly generous
God, the God who gives us everything: "he will take from what is mine
and declare it to you" (John 16:15).

ORDINARY TIME II

June 7, 2009

SOLEMNITY OF THE MOST HOLY TRINITY

A reading from the holy Gospel according to Matthew   *28:16–20*

The eleven disciples went to Galilee,
    to the mountain to which Jesus had ordered them.
When they all saw him, they worshiped,
    but they doubted.
Then Jesus approached and said to them,
    "All power in heaven and on earth has been
       given to me.
Go, therefore, and make disciples of all nations,
    baptizing them in the name of the Father,
    and of the Son, and of the Holy Spirit,
    teaching them to observe all that I have
       commanded you.
And behold, I am with you always, until the end
    of the age."

The Gospel of the Lord.

Reflection upon the power of God seen in the Resurrection of Christ engenders awe and wonder. Meditation upon the effect of Baptism bringing us into union with the Father, Son, and Holy Spirit inspires awe and wonder. The realization that Christ's call to discipleship is given to all the baptized is overwhelming. Christ's promise that he will be with us always inspires us to respond in faith and trust to fulfill our potential.

June 14, 2009

SOLEMNITY OF THE MOST HOLY BODY AND BLOOD OF CHRIST

A reading from the holy Gospel according to Mark
14:12–16, 22–26

On the first day of the Feast of Unleavened Bread,
    when they sacrificed the Passover lamb,
    Jesus' disciples said to him,
    "Where do you want us to go
    and prepare for you to eat the Passover?"
He sent two of his disciples and said to them,
    "Go into the city and a man will meet you,
    carrying a jar of water.
Follow him.
Wherever he enters, say to the master of the house,
    'The Teacher says, "Where is my guest room
    where I may eat the Passover with my disciples?"'
Then he will show you a large upper room furnished
        and ready.
Make the preparations for us there."

The disciples then went off, entered the city,
 and found it just as he had told them;
 and they prepared the Passover.

While they were eating,
 he took bread, said the blessing,
 broke it, gave it to them, and said,
 "Take it; this is my body."
Then he took a cup, gave thanks, and gave it to them,
 and they all drank from it.
He said to them,
 "This is my blood of the covenant,
 which will be shed for many.
Amen, I say to you,
 I shall not drink again the fruit of the vine
 until the day when I drink it new in the kingdom
  of God."
Then, after singing a hymn,
 they went out to the Mount of Olives.

The Gospel of the Lord.

EXPLANATION OF THE READING

There are many who struggle to understand how simple gifts of bread and
wine can become the true body and blood, soul and divinity of our Savior,
Jesus Christ. Yes, Eucharist requires us to have deep faith and to
acknowledge that our God is a God of mystery—a mystery so great it is
beyond understanding. Eucharist is an amazing experience of God's
presence. The sacrament reveals to us that God is powerful, faithful to his
promises, and so loving that he transforms these simple gifts into the most
life-giving manna we will ever consume; thus, filled with his holy
presence. We need not be consumed with the "how's" of this mystery; we
just need to believe that God indeed becomes the life-giving sacrament
that transforms our lives.

June 21, 2009

TWELFTH SUNDAY IN ORDINARY TIME

A reading from the holy Gospel according to Mark

4:35–41

On that day, as evening drew on, Jesus said
    to his disciples:
  "Let us cross to the other side."
Leaving the crowd, they took Jesus with them
    in the boat just as he was.
And other boats were with him.
A violent squall came up and waves were breaking
    over the boat,
  so that it was already filling up.
Jesus was in the stern, asleep on a cushion.
They woke him and said to him,
  "Teacher, do you not care that we are perishing?"
He woke up,
  rebuked the wind, and said to the sea,
    "Quiet! Be still!"
The wind ceased and there was great calm.
Then he asked them, "Why are you terrified?
Do you not yet have faith?"
They were filled with great awe and said
    to one another,
  "Who then is this whom even wind and sea obey?"

The Gospel of the Lord.

EXPLANATION OF THE READING

When times are difficult and our prayers seemingly go unanswered, we may be tempted to turn to God and ask, "Do you not care that we are perishing?" Today's Gospel reminds us that God does care. In the midst of turmoil, Christ whispers to us, "Be still. Do not be afraid. Have faith." God has not forgotten or abandoned us. If we can quiet ourselves long enough to let go and, in faith, submit to the will of God, we will find that the storms of our lives have been calmed.

June 28, 2009

THIRTEENTH SUNDAY IN ORDINARY TIME

A reading from the holy Gospel according to Mark   *5:21–24, 35b–43*

When Jesus had crossed again in the boat
   to the other side,
   a large crowd gathered around him,
      and he stayed close to the sea.
One of the synagogue officials, named Jairus,
      came forward.
Seeing him he fell at his feet and pleaded earnestly
      with him, saying,
   "My daughter is at the point of death.
Please, come lay your hands on her
      that she may get well and live."
He went off with him,
   and a large crowd followed him and pressed
      upon him.

While he was still speaking,
  people from the synagogue official's house
    arrived and said,
  "Your daughter has died; why trouble the teacher
    any longer?"
Disregarding the message that was reported,
  Jesus said to the synagogue official,
  "Do not be afraid; just have faith."
He did not allow anyone to accompany him inside
  except Peter, James, and John, the brother of James.
When they arrived at the house of
    the synagogue official,
  he caught sight of a commotion,
  people weeping and wailing loudly.
So he went in and said to them,
  "Why this commotion and weeping?
The child is not dead but asleep."
And they ridiculed him.
Then he put them all out.
He took along the child's father and mother
  and those who were with him
  and entered the room where the child was.
He took the child by the hand and said to her,
  "Talitha koum,"
  which means, "Little girl, I say to you, arise!"
The girl, a child of twelve, arose immediately and
  walked around.
At that they were utterly astounded.

He gave strict orders that no one should know this
   and said that she should be given something to eat.

The Gospel of the Lord.

Longer form: Mark 5:21–43

EXPLANATION OF THE READING

The woman with the hemorrhage and the official both approach the Lord
with great trust in his ability to heal. We, too, can approach the Lord with
a trust that proclaims, "Lord, I know you will fulfill that which I need." We
don't need to ask if the Lord can provide for us; we know he can provide
for us, and we trust he will provide for us, his beloved children. Our God
loves us and will care for us always.

July 5, 2009

FOURTEENTH SUNDAY IN ORDINARY TIME

A reading from the holy Gospel according to Mark   6:1–6a

Jesus departed from there and came to his native place,
   accompanied by his disciples.
When the sabbath came he began to teach
   in the synagogue,
   and many who heard him were astonished.
They said, "Where did this man get all this?
What kind of wisdom has been given him?
What mighty deeds are wrought by his hands!

Is he not the carpenter, the son of Mary,
  and the brother of James and Joses and Judas
    and Simon?
And are not his sisters here with us?"
And they took offense at him.
Jesus said to them,
  "A prophet is not without honor except in
    his native place
  and among his own kin and in his own house."
So he was not able to perform any mighty deed there,
  apart from curing a few sick people by laying
    his hands on them.
He was amazed at their lack of faith.

The Gospel of the Lord.

EXPLANATION OF THE READING

Last week, Jesus worked two wonders of healing; this week, he brings his
glad tidings to his own native place and finds the people unwilling to listen
to him. They know that they are hearing something extraordinary:
"Where did this man get all this?" (Mark 6:2) they ask. Although they
recognize his wisdom, they do not allow it to touch their hearts. These are
the people Jesus grew up with—his own family and friends, those who
should know him best; and they reject him. No wonder Jesus is amazed at
their lack of faith. This is the only place in the Gospel where it says that
Jesus "was not able" (Mark 6:5). Without their faith, Jesus cannot work
wonders among them. This passage foreshadows Jesus' approaching
Passion, when even his disciples will desert him.

July 12, 2009

Fifteenth Sunday in Ordinary Time

A reading from the holy Gospel according to Mark

6:7–13

Jesus summoned the Twelve and began to send them
    out two by two
  and gave them authority over unclean spirits.
He instructed them to take nothing for the journey
    but a walking stick—
  no food, no sack, no money in their belts.
They were, however, to wear sandals
  but not a second tunic.
He said to them,
    "Wherever you enter a house, stay there until
        you leave.
Whatever place does not welcome you or listen to you,
    leave there and shake the dust off your feet
  in testimony against them."
So they went off and preached repentance.
The Twelve drove out many demons,
    and they anointed with oil many who were sick
        and cured them.

The Gospel of the Lord.

Explanation of the Reading

In the Gospel, we hear Mark's account of the sending of the Twelve. Jesus
sends them forth, two by two, to do exactly what he has done: cast out
demons, heal the sick, and preach repentance. They are to travel light.
They are not even to take a change of clothes. It is not that the apostles

won't need anything, but by not providing for themselves, they are trusting in the Lord and in the kindness of strangers to provide for them. This must have been a difficult act of faith for these men used to earning their keep. Even harder, perhaps, is how they are to respond when people disagree with them. They are not to argue it out or to become angry; they are simply to walk away. Two thousand years later, the followers of Christ don't find that advice any easier to follow.

July 19, 2009

SIXTEENTH SUNDAY IN ORDINARY TIME

A reading from the holy Gospel according to Mark

6:30–34

The apostles gathered together with Jesus
    and reported all they had done and taught.
He said to them,
    "Come away by yourselves to a deserted place and
        rest a while."
People were coming and going in great numbers,
    and they had no opportunity even to eat.
So they went off in the boat by themselves
    to a deserted place.
People saw them leaving and many came to know
    about it.
They hastened there on foot from all the towns
    and arrived at the place before them.

When he disembarked and saw the vast crowd,
    his heart was moved with pity for them,

for they were like sheep without a shepherd;
and he began to teach them many things.

The Gospel of the Lord.

EXPLANATION OF THE READING

Jesus is tired. No wonder. He's been moving nonstop, calming the wind
and the waves, healing, teaching, and casting out demons. Now he invites
his disciples to come away and "rest awhile" (Mark 6:31). But word of his
departure leaks out, and people start moving. When Jesus reaches the
"deserted place" (Mark 6:32), he finds a "vast crowd" (Mark 6:34). The
compassionate heart of Jesus is touched at once, and he changes his
plans. These "sheep without a shepherd" (ibid.) need him, and he teaches
them "many things" (ibid.).

July 26, 2009

SEVENTEENTH SUNDAY IN ORDINARY TIME

A reading from the holy Gospel according to John

6:1–15

Jesus went across the Sea of Galilee.
A large crowd followed him,
    because they saw the signs he was performing
        on the sick.
Jesus went up on the mountain,
    and there he sat down with his disciples.
The Jewish feast of Passover was near.
When Jesus raised his eyes
    and saw that a large crowd was coming to him,

he said to Philip,
    "Where can we buy enough food for them to eat?"
He said this to test him,
    because he himself knew what he was going to do.
Philip answered him,
    "Two hundred days' wages worth of food
        would not be enough
    for each of them to have a little."
One of his disciples,
    Andrew, the brother of Simon Peter, said to him,
    "There is a boy here who has five barley loaves and
        two fish;
    but what good are these for so many?"
Jesus said, "Have the people recline."
Now there was a great deal of grass in that place.
So the men reclined, about five thousand in number.
Then Jesus took the loaves, gave thanks,
    and distributed them to those who were reclining,
    and also as much of the fish as they wanted.
When they had had their fill, he said to his disciples,
    "Gather the fragments left over,
    so that nothing will be wasted."
So they collected them,
    and filled twelve wicker baskets with fragments
    from the five barley loaves
    that had been more than they could eat.
When the people saw the sign he had done, they said,
    "This is truly the Prophet, the one who is to come
        into the world."

Since Jesus knew that they were going to come and
    carry him off
  to make him king,
  he withdrew again to the mountain alone.

The Gospel of the Lord.

EXPLANATION OF THE READING

Here are five thousand men (we can only imagine that, with the women
and children, the actual number present was much larger). A child is the
only one who seems to have brought anything to eat; he gives his five
loaves and two fish to the disciples. Jesus blesses this tiny offering, and
the disciples carry the food to the people. It is not in the blessing but in
the distribution that the miracle occurs. The abundance is so great that
twelve baskets of fragments are left over after all have eaten their fill. The
people see only the surface of the mystery, and of course they want to
make Jesus their king. Imagine a king who can make something out of
nothing, who can miraculously supply all their wants! But Jesus slips
away to the mountain, alone.

August 2, 2009

EIGHTEENTH SUNDAY
IN ORDINARY TIME

A reading from the holy Gospel
according to John   6:24–35

When the crowd saw that neither Jesus nor
    his disciples were there,
  they themselves got into boats
  and came to Capernaum looking for Jesus.

And when they found him across the sea they
    said to him,
  "Rabbi, when did you get here?"
Jesus answered them and said,
  "Amen, amen, I say to you,
  you are looking for me not because you saw signs
  but because you ate the loaves and were filled.
Do not work for food that perishes
  but for the food that endures for eternal life,
  which the Son of Man will give you.
For on him the Father, God, has set his seal."
So they said to him,
  "What can we do to accomplish the works of God?"
Jesus answered and said to them,
  "This is the work of God, that you believe in
    the one he sent."
So they said to him,
  "What sign can you do, that we may see and
    believe in you?
What can you do?
Our ancestors ate manna in the desert, as it is written:
  He gave them bread from heaven to eat."
So Jesus said to them,
  "Amen, amen, I say to you,
  it was not Moses who gave the bread from heaven;
  my Father gives you the true bread from heaven.
For the bread of God is that which comes down
    from heaven
  and gives life to the world."

So they said to him,
    "Sir, give us this bread always."
Jesus said to them,
    "I am the bread of life;
    whoever comes to me will never hunger,
    and whoever believes in me will never thirst."

The Gospel of the Lord.

EXPLANATION OF THE READING

There truly is a lot for us to chew on in today's Gospel. But puns about bread aside, perhaps the best place to start is with Jesus' reminder, "This is the work of God, that you believe in the one he sent." Our main mission, then, should we choose to accept it, is simply to have faith and believe in Jesus Christ as the Son of God. If we truly believe, then we do not need signs and wonders to prove Jesus' power, and we will not get caught up in striving for earthly pleasures. If we truly believe, then we understand in our very core that Jesus is all we need. He is the bread of life who fills our every need and desire. In Christ, we will never hunger. In Christ, we will have eternal life.

August 9, 2009

NINETEENTH SUNDAY IN ORDINARY TIME

A reading from the holy Gospel according to John
6:41–51

The Jews murmured about Jesus because he said,
    "I am the bread that came down from heaven,"
    and they said,
    "Is this not Jesus, the son of Joseph?
Do we not know his father and mother?

Then how can he say,
  'I have come down from heaven'?"
Jesus answered and said to them,
  "Stop murmuring among yourselves.
No one can come to me unless the Father who sent
    me draw him,
  and I will raise him on the last day.
It is written in the prophets:
  They shall all be taught by God.
Everyone who listens to my Father and learns
    from him comes to me.
Not that anyone has seen the Father
  except the one who is from God;
  he has seen the Father.
Amen, amen, I say to you,
  whoever believes has eternal life.
I am the bread of life.
Your ancestors ate the manna in the desert,
    but they died;
  this is the bread that comes down from heaven
  so that one may eat it and not die.
I am the living bread that came down from heaven;
  whoever eats this bread will live forever;
  and the bread that I will give is my flesh for the life
    of the world."

The Gospel of the Lord.

EXPLANATION OF THE READING

Some of the Jews clearly don't want to accept Jesus as being necessary
to their lives. They ridicule the very idea that he has come down from

heaven. They know better. They know his parents. How dare he assume the role of God who fed their ancestors in the desert! Yet Jesus persists in his self-revelation as living bread for the life of the world. The Eucharist we receive is the very person of Jesus, a gift beyond imagining. He offers himself that we may live forever.

August 16, 2009

TWENTIETH SUNDAY IN ORDINARY TIME

A reading from the holy Gospel according to John

6:51–58

Jesus said to the crowds:
  "I am the living bread that came down from heaven;
  whoever eats this bread will live forever;
  and the bread that I will give
  is my flesh for the life of the world."

The Jews quarreled among themselves, saying,
  "How can this man give us his flesh to eat?"
Jesus said to them,
  "Amen, amen, I say to you,
  unless you eat the flesh of the Son of Man and
    drink his blood,
  you do not have life within you.
Whoever eats my flesh and drinks my blood
  has eternal life,
  and I will raise him on the last day.

For my flesh is true food,
  and my blood is true drink.
Whoever eats my flesh and drinks my blood
  remains in me and I in him.
Just as the living Father sent me
  and I have life because of the Father,
  so also the one who feeds on me
  will have life because of me.
This is the bread that came down from heaven.
Unlike your ancestors who ate and still died,
  whoever eats this bread will live forever."

The Gospel of the Lord.

EXPLANATION OF THE READING

Most of Chapter Six of the Gospel according to John is known as the Bread of Life discourse. John reports that this teaching of Jesus was delivered in the synagogue of Capernaum. The crowd of people who first heard these words of Jesus were astounded and angry; they even quarreled among themselves. We don't really know why they reacted this way or why they felt threatened by such a teaching. What is more important is how we react to and accept what Jesus said. This passage is at the heart of our Eucharistic theology, and our only response ought to be one of immense gratitude. The promise of Jesus to those who eat his flesh and drink his blood is the gift of eternal life. We know that Jesus speaks in a language beneath the literal sense of these words; we know that what he speaks of rests in the very mystery of God. We cannot fully understand this, and it is only with the eyes and heart of faith that we can be open to the magnitude of this promise. As we approach the banquet table of the Eucharist, we might be overwhelmed at the thought of receiving this "true bread" and "true drink," but being overwhelmed is the beginning of gratitude, and that is the only appropriate posture before the Lord.

August 23, 2009

Twenty-first Sunday
in Ordinary Time

A reading from the holy Gospel
according to John   6:60–69

Many of Jesus' disciples who were listening said,
  "This saying is hard; who can accept it?"
Since Jesus knew that his disciples were murmuring
    about this,
  he said to them, "Does this shock you?
What if you were to see the Son of Man ascending
  to where he was before?
It is the spirit that gives life,
  while the flesh is of no avail.
The words I have spoken to you are Spirit and life.
But there are some of you who do not believe."
Jesus knew from the beginning the ones who
    would not believe
  and the one who would betray him.
And he said,
  "For this reason I have told you that no one can
    come to me
  unless it is granted him by my Father."

As a result of this,
  many of his disciples returned to their former way
    of life
  and no longer accompanied him.

Jesus then said to the Twelve, "Do you also want
   to leave?"
Simon Peter answered him, "Master, to whom shall
   we go?
You have the words of eternal life.
We have come to believe
   and are convinced that you are the Holy One
   of God."

The Gospel of the Lord.

EXPLANATION OF THE READING

Jesus has finished telling the disciples that he is the bread of life come
down from heaven, and that his flesh is real food and his blood is real
drink. Furthermore, whoever eats this bread will live forever. One can only
imagine that this was a shocking revelation and how hard it was for the
disciples to accept. The mystery and the sacrament of Eucharist are
founded in this great teaching of Jesus. When we think seriously about the
Eucharistic presence of Christ, it can be rather frightening and difficult to
grasp. Not frightening as to scare us, but as to cause us to be in awe of
"so great a gift." And we might well wonder, if I accept this truth, how will
I live it? How do I give thanks for such a profound grace? The choice of the
disciple is indeed a hard choice, but not one without the loving support of
the Lord that we celebrate at every Eucharist. Peter made such a choice
and said to Jesus: "To whom [else] shall we go? You have the words of
eternal life." We need to think like Peter today.

August 30, 2009

Twenty-second Sunday
in Ordinary Time

A reading from the holy Gospel according to Mark   *7:1–8, 14–15, 21–23*

When the Pharisees with some scribes who had
    come from Jerusalem
  gathered around Jesus,
  they observed that some of his disciples
    ate their meals
with unclean, that is, unwashed, hands.
—For the Pharisees and, in fact, all Jews,
  do not eat without carefully washing their hands,
  keeping the tradition of the elders.
And on coming from the marketplace
  they do not eat without purifying themselves.
And there are many other things that they have
    traditionally observed,
  the purification of cups and jugs and kettles
    and beds.—
So the Pharisees and scribes questioned him,
  "Why do your disciples not follow the tradition
    of the elders
  but instead eat a meal with unclean hands?"
He responded,
  "Well did Isaiah prophesy about you hypocrites,
    as it is written:

> This people honors me with their lips,
>> but their hearts are far from me;
> in vain do they worship me,
>> teaching as doctrines human precepts.

You disregard God's commandment but cling to
   human tradition."
He summoned the crowd again and said to them,
   "Hear me, all of you, and understand.
Nothing that enters one from outside can defile
   that person;
   but the things that come out from within are
   what defile.

"From within people, from their hearts,
   come evil thoughts, unchastity, theft, murder,
   adultery, greed, malice, deceit,
   licentiousness, envy, blasphemy, arrogance, folly.
All these evils come from within and they defile."

The Gospel of the Lord.

EXPLANATION OF THE READING

In a very true sense, the teaching of Jesus in this passage gets to the heart
of the matter. He uses a simple and ordinary ritual of hand-washing
before meals to get beneath the meaning of ritual customs, pointing out
that human custom does not matter if the person's heart is not focused on
the real purpose of the custom. All human actions, Jesus says, are to bring
honor to God. And he quotes Isaiah to remind the Pharisees that
generations before them were just like them. They honored God with their
lips, but their hearts were "far from me." In other words, their words and
actions were shallow and insincere, even though they did the correct thing
to speak of God in an honorable way. So, too, those to whom Jesus speaks;
they do the correct thing but only for the sake of the human tradition and
recognition, not for the glory of God. It can be the same with us; we "go

through the motions," but our hearts are not in the right place. True motive resides in the heart, and true love of God and of neighbor begins with a heart full of sincerity.

September 6, 2009

TWENTY-THIRD SUNDAY IN ORDINARY TIME

A reading from the holy Gospel according to Mark 7:31–37

Again Jesus left the district of Tyre
    and went by way of Sidon to the Sea of Galilee,
    into the district of the Decapolis.
And people brought to him a deaf man who had
     a speech impediment
    and begged him to lay his hand on him.
He took him off by himself away from the crowd.
He put his finger into the man's ears
    and, spitting, touched his tongue;
    then he looked up to heaven and groaned,
     and said to him,
    "Ephphatha!"—that is, "Be opened!"—
And immediately the man's ears were opened,
    his speech impediment was removed,
    and he spoke plainly.
He ordered them not to tell anyone.
But the more he ordered them not to,
    the more they proclaimed it.

They were exceedingly astonished and they said,
   "He has done all things well.
He makes the deaf hear and the mute speak."

The Gospel of the Lord.

EXPLANATION OF THE READING

Sharing our faith is not always easy. We hold back because we are fearful
of judgment, or we may not know enough about our beliefs. Whatever the
reason, we need to view our faith as a gift meant to be shared. We have
the responsibility to help it grow. We are called to constantly learn about
God and his commands. We are also called to reflect upon the ways in
which we hide our faith. What would it be like to be so excited by Christ's
healing power—as were those in the Gospel—that we were unable to
contain our excitement? What would we proclaim?

September 13, 2009

TWENTY-FOURTH SUNDAY IN ORDINARY TIME

A reading from the holy Gospel according to Mark
8:27–35

Jesus and his disciples set out
   for the villages of Caesarea Philippi.
Along the way he asked his disciples,
   "Who do people say that I am?"
They said in reply,
   "John the Baptist, others Elijah,
   still others one of the prophets."
And he asked them,
   "But who do you say that I am?"

Peter said to him in reply,
  "You are the Christ."
Then he warned them not to tell anyone about him.

He began to teach them
    that the Son of Man must suffer greatly
    and be rejected by the elders, the chief priests,
        and the scribes,
    and be killed, and rise after three days.
He spoke this openly.
Then Peter took him aside and began to rebuke him.
At this he turned around and, looking at his disciples,
    rebuked Peter and said, "Get behind me, Satan.
You are thinking not as God does, but as
        human beings do."

He summoned the crowd with his disciples and
        said to them,
    "Whoever wishes to come after me must
        deny himself,
    take up his cross, and follow me.
For whoever wishes to save his life will lose it,
    but whoever loses his life for my sake
    and that of the gospel will save it."

The Gospel of the Lord.

EXPLANATION OF THE READING

Peter's rebuttal against the suffering and death of the Messiah is linked to
an even deeper fear; if even the Christ must suffer and die, then I too must
suffer and die. Christ's suffering and death reveals the Messiah has the

power to transform suffering and death into life. It is with hope then that we can reflect on the sufferings Christ has transformed in our own lives and ask him for the faith to endure those things we are now suffering with and will suffer.

September 20, 2009

TWENTY-FIFTH SUNDAY IN ORDINARY TIME

A reading from the holy Gospel according to Mark   9:30–37

Jesus and his disciples left from there and began
    a journey through Galilee,
  but he did not wish anyone to know about it.
He was teaching his disciples and telling them,
    "The Son of Man is to be handed over to men
    and they will kill him,
    and three days after his death the Son of Man
        will rise."
But they did not understand the saying,
    and they were afraid to question him.

They came to Capernaum and, once inside the house,
    he began to ask them,
    "What were you arguing about on the way?"
But they remained silent.
They had been discussing among themselves
        on the way
    who was the greatest.

Then he sat down, called the Twelve, and said to them,
"If anyone wishes to be first,
he shall be the last of all and the servant of all."
Taking a child, he placed it in their midst,
and putting his arms around it, he said to them,
"Whoever receives one child such as this in
my name, receives me;
and whoever receives me,
receives not me but the One who sent me."

The Gospel of the Lord.

EXPLANATION OF THE READING

The love of Christ is beyond comprehension—just look at Jesus' response to the disciples. Jesus tells the disciples he will die and rise again. Instead of feeling sadness or a sense of awe, the disciples argue over who is the greatest. But despite their callousness, Jesus does not turn them away. Rather, he tries to help them see that love, not pride, and service to others is the way of God. Let us reflect on the ways in which our God loves us despite our pride and lack of understanding.

September 27, 2009

TWENTY-SIXTH SUNDAY IN ORDINARY TIME

A reading from the holy Gospel according to Mark
9:38–43, 45, 47–48

At that time, John said to Jesus,
"Teacher, we saw someone driving out demons
in your name,

and we tried to prevent him because he does not
    follow us."
Jesus replied, "Do not prevent him.
There is no one who performs a mighty deed
    in my name
    who can at the same time speak ill of me.
For whoever is not against us is for us.
Anyone who gives you a cup of water to drink
    because you belong to Christ,
    amen, I say to you, will surely not lose his reward.

"Whoever causes one of these little ones
    who believe in me to sin,
    it would be better for him if a great millstone
    were put around his neck
    and he were thrown into the sea.
If your hand causes you to sin, cut it off.
It is better for you to enter into life maimed
    than with two hands to go into Gehenna,
    into the unquenchable fire.
And if your foot causes you to sin, cut it off.
It is better for you to enter into life crippled
    than with two feet to be thrown into Gehenna.
And if your eye causes you to sin, pluck it out.
Better for you to enter into the kingdom of God
    with one eye
    than with two eyes to be thrown into Gehenna,

where 'their worm does not die, and the fire
　　is not quenched.' "

The Gospel of the Lord.

EXPLANATION OF THE READING

Although God continues to love us even when we sin, sin disrupts our
relationship with him. Over time, the sins that we consciously choose to
commit become routine. Sinful actions may become habitual, and we may
no longer be conscious that our actions are wrong. Turning from sin can
be as difficult as it would be to cut off one's hand or to pluck out ones eye.
If we are to grow in love, we must begin the hard task of examining our
actions. We can start by actively stopping those sins that we know are
wrong and seek God's guidance and forgiveness. Today let us examine
what we need to cut off or pluck out of our lives in order to become closer
to God.

October 4, 2009

TWENTY-SEVENTH SUNDAY
IN ORDINARY TIME

A reading from the holy Gospel
according to Mark
10:2–16

The Pharisees approached Jesus and asked,
　　"Is it lawful for a husband to divorce his wife?"
They were testing him.
He said to them in reply, "What did Moses
　　command you?"
They replied,
　　"Moses permitted a husband to write a bill
　　　of divorce
　　and dismiss her."

But Jesus told them,
  "Because of the hardness of your hearts
  he wrote you this commandment.
But from the beginning of creation, *God made them
    male and female.*
*For this reason a man shall leave his father and mother
    and be joined to his wife,
    and the two shall become one flesh.*
So they are no longer two but one flesh.
Therefore what God has joined together,
    no human being must separate."
In the house the disciples again questioned Jesus
    about this.
He said to them,
  "Whoever divorces his wife and marries another
  commits adultery against her;
  and if she divorces her husband and marries another,
  she commits adultery."

And people were bringing children to him
    that he might touch them,
  but the disciples rebuked them.
When Jesus saw this he became indignant and said
    to them,
  "Let the children come to me;
  do not prevent them, for the kingdom of God
    belongs to such as these.

Amen, I say to you,
   whoever does not accept the kingdom of God
      like a child
   will not enter it."
Then he embraced them and blessed them,
   placing his hands on them.

The Gospel of the Lord.

EXPLANATION OF THE READING

Once again the disciples are confused with Jesus' role in the world. They rebuke the children from coming to him because they believe that someone as important as Jesus does not have time to waste on a child. But Jesus' words are clear. Children should be allowed to approach Jesus just as an adult would. In fact, an adult should follow the way of the child. Imagine adults being told that the kingdom of God belongs to children! But this is exactly what Jesus does. His message is that people of all ages need the presence of Christ, and that Christ is constantly calling those we do not consider worthy into his kingdom. Today let us pray for those people who are often judged unworthy of Christ and for the child-like faith we need to approach Christ.

October 11, 2009

TWENTY-EIGHTH SUNDAY IN ORDINARY TIME

A reading from the holy Gospel according to Mark

10:17–27

As Jesus was setting out on a journey, a man ran up,
   knelt down before him, and asked him,
   "Good teacher, what must I do to inherit
      eternal life?"

Jesus answered him, "Why do you call me good?
No one is good but God alone.
You know the commandments: *You shall not kill;*
 you shall not commit adultery;
 you shall not steal;
 you shall not bear false witness;
 you shall not defraud;
 honor your father and your mother."
He replied and said to him,
 "Teacher, all of these I have observed from
 my youth."
Jesus, looking at him, loved him and said to him,
 "You are lacking in one thing.
Go, sell what you have, and give to the poor
 and you will have treasure in heaven; then come,
 follow me."
At that statement his face fell,
 and he went away sad, for he had many possessions.

Jesus looked around and said to his disciples,
 "How hard it is for those who have wealth
 to enter the kingdom of God!"
The disciples were amazed at his words.
So Jesus again said to them in reply,
 "Children, how hard it is to enter the kingdom
 of God!

It is easier for a camel to pass through the eye
    of a needle
  than for one who is rich to enter the kingdom
    of God."
They were exceedingly astonished and said
    among themselves,
  "Then who can be saved?"
Jesus looked at them and said,
  "For human beings it is impossible, but not for God.
All things are possible for God."

The Gospel of the Lord.

Longer form: Mark 10:17–30

EXPLANATION OF THE READING

Can we posses many things and still follow God? The person unable to
enter heaven is not the rich person, but the one who allows his or her
possessions to be of more importance than God and neighbor. Surely,
what we give up in this life to follow Christ's commands will be returned
to us a hundredfold when we enter the kingdom of heaven. Surely, our
acts of justice and mercy will have more of an effect when we align our
wills and actions with God.

October 18, 2009

Twenty-ninth Sunday in Ordinary Time

A reading from the holy Gospel according to Mark

10:42–45

Jesus summoned the Twelve and said to them,
> "You know that those who are recognized as rulers
>   over the Gentiles
> lord it over them,
> and their great ones make their authority over
>   them felt.
> But it shall not be so among you.
> Rather, whoever wishes to be great among you will
>   be your servant;
> whoever wishes to be first among you will be
>   the slave of all.
> For the Son of Man did not come to be served
>   but to serve and to give his life as a ransom
>   for many."

The Gospel of the Lord.

Longer form: Mark 10:35–45

EXPLANATION OF THE READING

The things we have in life can bring us great joy and pleasure, but they also bring great responsibility. No one has experienced as much responsibility as Jesus. He allowed himself to suffer and die, so that we could live. And while we, like the disciples, can never fully understand the depth of Christ's love for us, we must seek to embrace the responsibility God has given us as a sign of our thankfulness to God.

October 25, 2009

THIRTIETH SUNDAY IN ORDINARY TIME

A reading from the holy Gospel according to Mark

10:46–52

As Jesus was leaving Jericho with his disciples and
    a sizable crowd,
  Bartimaeus, a blind man, the son of Timaeus,
  sat by the roadside begging.
On hearing that it was Jesus of Nazareth,
  he began to cry out and say,
  "Jesus, son of David, have pity on me."
And many rebuked him, telling him to be silent.
But he kept calling out all the more,
  "Son of David, have pity on me."
Jesus stopped and said, "Call him."
So they called the blind man, saying to him,
  "Take courage; get up, Jesus is calling you."
He threw aside his cloak, sprang up, and came
    to Jesus.
Jesus said to him in reply, "What do you want me
    to do for you?"
The blind man replied to him, "Master, I want to see."
Jesus told him, "Go your way; your faith has
    saved you."
Immediately he received his sight
  and followed him on the way.

The Gospel of the Lord.

Explanation of the Reading

Like Bartimaeus, we have not directly seen the miracles of Christ, but in faith we believe. There are people in the world who think that faith is really a form of naïveté. These are people who want the hard facts and want to see for themselves, but they are the ones who are missing out on the gift that is faith. Take Bartimaeus, for example. He could have chosen not to believe the stories about Jesus, only to spend the rest of his life on the side of the road blindly begging. Instead he called out, asked for the Lord's healing, and in that moment everything changed. Today let us consider the things that God could heal or change in our lives if only we called out to him in faith.

November 1, 2009

Solemnity of All Saints

A reading from the holy Gospel according to Matthew

5:1–12a

When Jesus saw the crowds, he went up the
    mountain,
  and after he had sat down, his disciples came to him.
He began to teach them, saying:

  "Blessed are the poor in spirit,
    for theirs is the Kingdom of heaven.
  Blessed are they who mourn,
    for they will be comforted.
  Blessed are the meek,
    for they will inherit the land.
  Blessed are they who hunger and thirst
    for righteousness,
      for they will be satisfied.

Blessed are the merciful,
  for they will be shown mercy.
Blessed are the clean of heart,
  for they will see God.
Blessed are the peacemakers,
  for they will be called children of God.
Blessed are they who are persecuted for the sake
    of righteousness,
  for theirs is the Kingdom of heaven.
Blessed are you when they insult you and
    persecute you
    and utter every kind of evil against you falsely
    because of me.
Rejoice and be glad,
  for your reward will be great in heaven."

The Gospel of the Lord.

EXPLANATION OF THE READING

Christ brings a new prioritization for life. The things we thought were important are now cast in a different light. Money, power, and a good reputation mean nothing if they keep us from God and from his kingdom. We are not naïve in knowing that following Christ is difficult. Faith in Christ may be mocked in this life, but it will not go unnoticed.

November 8, 2009

Thirty-second Sunday in Ordinary Time

A reading from the holy Gospel according to Mark
12:41–44

Jesus sat down opposite the treasury
 and observed how the crowd put money
  into the treasury.
Many rich people put in large sums.
A poor widow also came and put in two small coins
 worth a few cents.
Calling his disciples to himself, he said to them,
 "Amen, I say to you, this poor widow put in more
 than all the other contributors to the treasury.
For they have all contributed from their surplus wealth,
 but she, from her poverty, has contributed
  all she had,
 her whole livelihood."

The Gospel of the Lord.

Longer form: Mark 12:38–44

Explanation of the Reading

In today's Gospel, the poor widow is recognized by Christ as the one who gave the most—not because she was wealthy and gave the most money, but because she gave freely and probably more than she could afford to give. While her offering may not go far in sustaining the cost to run the temple, her offering shows the scribes the true sacrifice that Christ calls us to make. Today let us consider all the ways in which we give to others and consider all the things that we are not sharing with the world.

November 15, 2009

THIRTY-THIRD SUNDAY IN ORDINARY TIME

A reading from the holy Gospel according to Mark

13:24–32

Jesus said to his disciples:
"In those days after that tribulation
   the sun will be darkened,
      and the moon will not give its light,
   and the stars will be falling from the sky,
      and the powers in the heavens will be shaken.

"And then they will see 'the Son of Man coming
      in the clouds'
   with great power and glory,
   and then he will send out the angels
   and gather his elect from the four winds,
   from the end of the earth to the end of the sky.

"Learn a lesson from the fig tree.
When its branch becomes tender and sprouts leaves,
   you know that summer is near.
In the same way, when you see these things happening,
   know that he is near, at the gates.
Amen, I say to you,
   this generation will not pass away
   until all these things have taken place.

Heaven and earth will pass away,
  but my words will not pass away.

"But of that day or hour, no one knows,
  neither the angels in heaven, nor the Son, but only
    the Father."

The Gospel of the Lord.

EXPLANATION OF THE READING

Stories of the end times are probably not what we like to hear. The sun
will be darkened, stars will fall from the sky, and heaven and earth will
shake. This does not sound like a peaceful return of Christ. But Jesus is
merciful. Yes, the Gospel stories about the end times can be frightening
because they make us look deeply at our faith and commitment to our
Lord. At the same time, however, the message of the Gospel is comforting
because it promises that our faith in Christ will not go unnoticed. Today
let us ask that our faith will be strengthened so that we may welcome and
not fear the coming of the kingdom of God.

November 22, 2009

SOLEMNITY OF OUR LORD
JESUS CHRIST THE KING

A reading from the holy Gospel
according to John

18:33b–37

Pilate said to Jesus,
  "Are you the King of the Jews?"
Jesus answered, "Do you say this on your own
  or have others told you about me?"
Pilate answered, "I am not a Jew, am I?

Your own nation and the chief priests handed you
	over to me.
What have you done?"
Jesus answered, "My kingdom does not belong
	to this world.
If my kingdom did belong to this world,
	my attendants would be fighting
	to keep me from being handed over to the Jews.
But as it is, my kingdom is not here."
So Pilate said to him, "Then you are a king?"
Jesus answered, "You say I am a king.
For this I was born and for this I came into the world,
	to testify to the truth.
Everyone who belongs to the truth listens to my voice."

The Gospel of the Lord.

EXPLANATION OF THE READING

The Gospel takes us back to Holy Week. In the acclamation, it is Palm
Sunday, and we shout, "blessed is the kingdom of our father David that is
to come!" (Mark 11:10). In the Gospel, we move to Good Friday, as we
read from Pilate's interrogation of Jesus in John's narrative. Pilate has
heard the accusations of the priests and scribes, and he wants to know
the facts. *Is Jesus the so-called "King of the Jews," or not (John 18:33)? It is
clear to this cunning leader that Jesus poses a political threat; otherwise, why
would his own people have handed him over?* Pilate utterly fails to understand
Jesus' answer: "My kingdom does not belong to this world. . . . my
kingdom is not here" (John 18:36). The literal-minded Pilate cannot see
that the man who stands before him is indeed a king, but a king of
paradox: his rule comes through obedience to his Father, his riches
through self-emptying, his glory through suffering.

Patron Saints

The saints and blesseds are our companions in prayer on our journey with Christ. Here we provide you with a list of health concerns and the saints chosen to intercede on a sick person's behalf before God the Father.

AILMENTS	SAINT(S)
A	
abdominal pains	Agapitus; Charles Borromeo; Emerentiana; Erasmus; Liborius
abortion, protection against	Catherine of Sweden
abuse victims	Adelaide; Agostina Pietrantoni; Fabiola; John Baptist de la Salle; Germaine Cousin; Godelieve; Jeanne de Lestonnac; Jeanne Marie de Maille; Joaquina Vedruna de Mas; Laura Vicuna; Margaret the Barefooted; Maria Bagnesi; Monica; Pharaildis; Rita of Cascia
AIDS patients	Aloysius Gonzaga; Therese of Lisieux; Peregrine Lazios
alcoholism	John of God; Martin of Tours; Matthias the Apostle; Monica; Urban of Langres
angina sufferers	Swithbert
appendicitis	Erasmus (Elmo)
apoplexy, apoplexies, stroke, stroke victims	Andrew Avellino; Wolfgang
arm pain; pain in the arms	Amalburga

B

babies	The Holy Innocents; Maximus; Nicholas of Tolentino; Philip of Zell
bacterial disease and infection	Agrippina
barren women	Anthony of Padua; Felicity
barrenness, against	Agatha; Anne; Anthony of Padua; Casilda of Toledo; Felicity; Fiacre; Francis of Paola; Giles; Henry II; Margaret of Antioch; Medard; Philomena; Rita of Cascia; Theobald Roggeri
birth complications, against	Ulric
birth pains	Erasmus
blind people, blindness	Catald; Cosmas and Damian; Dunstan; Lawrence the Illuminator; Leodegarius; Lucy; Lutgardis; Odila; Parasceva; Raphael the Archangel; Thomas the Apostle
blood donors	Our Lady of the Thorns
bodily ills, illness, sickness	Alphais; Alphonsa of India; Angela Merici; Angela Truszkowska; Arthelais; Bathild; Bernadette of Lourdes; Camillus of Lellis; Catherine del Ricci; Catherine of Siena; Drogo; Edel Quinn; Elizabeth of the Trinity; Gerard of Villamagna; Germaine Cousin; Gorgonia; Hugh of Lincoln; Isabella of France; Jacinta Marto; John of God; Julia Billiart; Julia Falconieri; Juliana of Nicomedia; Louis IX; Louise de Marillac; Lydwina of Schiedam; Maria Bagnesi; Maria Gabriella; Maria Mazzarello; Marie Rose Durocher; Mary Ann de Paredes; Mary Magdalen of Pazzi; Michael the Archangel; Our Lady of Lourdes; Paula Frassinetti; Peregrine

	Laziosi; Philomena; Rafka Al-Rayes; Raphael; Romula; Syncletica; Teresa of Avila; Teresa Valse Pantellini; Terese of the Andes; Therese of Lisieux
breast cancer	Agatha; Aldegundis; Giles; Peregrine
breast disease, against	Agatha
breastfeeding women	Giles
broken bones	Drogo; Stanislaus Kostka

C

cancer patients; against cancer	Aldegundis; Giles; James Salomone; Peregrine Laziosi
child abuse victims	Alodia; Germaine Cousin; Lufthild; Nunilo
childbirth	Erasmus; Gerard Majella; Leonard of Noblac; Lutgardis; Margaret (or Marina) of Antioch; Raymond Nonnatus
childhood diseases	Aldegundis; Pharaildis
childhood intestinal diseases	Erasmus
children, convulsive	Guy of Anderlecht; John the Baptist; Scholastica
children, death of	Alphonsa Hawthorne; Angela of Foligno; Clotilde; Conception Cabrera de Annida; Cyriacus of Iconium; Dorothy of Montau; Elizabeth of Hungary; Elizabeth Ann Seton; Felicity; Frances of Rome; Hedwig; Isidore the Farmer; Joaquina Vedruna de Mas; Julitta; Leopold the Good; Louis IX; Luchesius; Margaret of Scotland; Marguerite d'Youville; Matilda; Melania the Younger; Michelina; Nonna; Perpetua; Stephen of Hungary

children, sick	Beuno; Clement I; Hugh of Lincoln; Ubaldus Baldassini
children, stammering	Notkar Balbulus
colic	Agapitus; Charles Borremo; Emerentiana; Erasmus; Liborius
contagious diseases	Robert Bellarmine; Sebastian
consumption	Pantaleon; Therese of Liseux
convulsions	John the Baptist; Willibrord
coughs, against	Blaise; Quentin; Walburga
cramps, against	Cadoc of Llancarvan; Maurice; Pancras
cures from pain	Madron

D

deaf people, deafness	Cadoc of Llancarvan; Drogo; Francis de Sales; Meriadoc; Ouen
death	Michael the Archangel; Margaret (or Marina) of Antioch
death, happy	Joseph; Ulric
death, against sudden	Aldegundis; Andrew Avellino; Barbara; Christopher
disabled, handicapped	Alphais; Angela Merici; Gerald of Aurillac; Germaine Cousin; Giles; Henry II; Lutgardis; Margaret of Castello; Seraphina; Servatus; Servulus
drug abuse	Maximillian Kolbe
dying people, invoked by	Abel; Barbara; Benedict; Catherine of Alexandria; James the Lesser, Apostle; John of God; Joseph; Margaret (or Marina) of Antioch; Michael the Archangel; Nicholas of Tolentino; Sebastian

dysentary	Lucy of Syracuse; Polycarp

E

earache, against	Cornelius; Polycarp of Smyrna
epidemics	Godeberta; Lucy of Syracuse; Our Lady of Zapopan; Roch (Rocco)
epilepsy, epileptics	Alban of Mainz; Anthony the Abbot; Balthasar; Bibiana; Catald; Christopher; Cornelius; Dymphna; Genesius; Gerard of Lunel; Giles; Guy of Anderlecht; John Chrysostom; John the Baptist; Valentine; Vitus; Willibrord
ergotism, aginst	Anthony the Abbot
erysipelas	Anthony the Abbot; Benedict; Ida of Nivelles
expectant Mothers	Gerard Majella; Raymond Nonnatus
eyes, eye diseases, eye problems, sore eyes	Aloysius Gonzaga; Augustine of Hippo; Clare of Assisi; Cyriacus of Iconium; Erhard of Regensburg; Herve; Leodegarius; Lucy of Syracuse; Raphael the Archangel; Symphorian of Autun

F

fainting, faintness	Urban of Langres; Ursus of Ravenna; Valentine
fever, against	Abraham; Adalard; Amalberga; Andrew Abellon; Antoninus of Florence; Benedict; Castorus; Claudius; Cornelius; Dominic of Sora; Domitian of Huy; Four Crowned Martyrs; Genevieve; Gerebernus; Gertrude of Nivelles; Hugh of Cluny; Jodocus; Liborius; Mary of Oignies; Nicostratus; Peter the Apostle; Petronilla; Raymond Nonnatus; Severus

	of Avranches; Sigismund; Simpronian; Theobald Roggeri; Ulric; Winnoc
fistula	Fiacre
frenzy, against	Denis; Peter the Apostle; Ulric
foot problems; feet problems	Peter the Apostle; Servatus

G

gall stones	Benedict; Drogo; Florentius of Strasburg; Liborius
goiter	Blaise
gout, against; gout sufferers	Andrew the Apostle; Coloman; Gerebernus; Gregory the Great; Killian; Maurice; Maurus; Totman

H

hangovers	Bibiana
head injuries	John Licci
headaches	Acacius; Anastasius the Persian; Bibiana; Denis; Dionysius the Aeropagite; Gerard of Lunel; Gereon; Pancras; Stephen the Martyr; Teresa of Avila; William Firmatus
health	Infant Jesus of Prague
healthy throats	Andrew the Apostle; Blaise; Etheldreda; Godelieve; Ignatius of Antioch; Lucy of Syracuse; Swithbert
heart patients	John of God
hemorrhage	Lucy
hemorrhoid, piles	Fiacre
hernia	Alban of Mainz; Condrad Piacenzai; Cosmas and Damian; Drogo; Gummarus

herpes	George
hoarseness, against	Bernadine of Sienna; Maurus
hydrophobia (rabies)	Dominic de Silos; Guy of Anderlecht; Hubert of Liege; Otto of Bamberg; Sithney; Walburga

I

infertility, against	Agatha; Anne; Anthony of Padua; Casilda of Toledo; Felicity; Fiacre; Francis of Paola; Giles; Henry II; Margaret of Antioch; Medard; Philomena; Rita of Cascia; Theobald Roggeri
inflammatory disease	Benedict
intestinal diseases, against	Brice; Charles Borromeo; Emerentiana; Erasmus; Timonthy; Wolfgang
invalids, homebound	Roch (Rocco)

J

jauntice	Odilo

K

kidney disease, against	Benedict; Drogo; Margaret (or Marina) of Antioch; Ursus of Ravenna
kidney stones; gravel	Alban of Mainz
knee diseases or trouble	Roch (Rocco)

L

lame, the	Giles
leg diseases, leg trouble	Servatus
lepers, leprosy	George; Giles; Lazarus; Vincent de Paul
long life	Peter the Apostle
lumbago	Lawrence

M

mental illness	Benedict Joseph Labre; Bibiana; Christina the Astonishing; Drogo; Dymphna; Eustochium of Padua; Fillan; Giles; Job; Margaret of Cortona; Maria Fortunata Viti; Medard; Michelina; Osmund; Raphaela; Romanus of Condat; Veran
migraine	Gereon; Severus of Avranches; Ulbadus Baldassini
milk, loss of by nursing women	Margaret of Antioch
miscarriage, against	Catherine of Sienna; Catherine of Sweden; Eulalia
miscarriage prevention	Catherine of Sweeden
muteness	Drogo

N

near sightedness, short sightedness	Clarus; Abbot
nerve or neurological disease, against	Bartholomew the Apostle; Dymphna
nursing mothers	Concordia; Martina

O

obsession	Quirinus

P

pain relief	Madron
paralysis	Catald; Osmund; Wolfgang
physical spouse abuse, against; victims of spouse abuse, against	Rita of Cascia
plague, against	Adrian of Nicomedia; Catald; Colman of Stockerau; Cuthbert; Edmund of East

	Anglia; Erhard of Regensburg; Francis of Paola; Francis Xavier; George; Genevieve; Gregory the Great; Macarius of Antioch; Roch (Rocco); Sebastian; Valentine; Walburga
poison sufferers	Benedict; Abbot; John the Apostles; Pirmin
pregnant women, pregnancy	Anne; Anthony of Padua; Elizabeth; Gerard Majella; Joseph; Margaret (or Marina) of Antioch; Raymond Nonnatus; Ulric

R

rape victims	Agatha; Agnes of Rome; Antona Messina; Dymphna; Joan of Arc; Maria Goretti; Pierina Morosini; Potamiaena; Solange; Zita
rheumatism, arthritis	Alphonus Maria de Liguori; Coloman; James the Greater; Killian; Servatus; Totnan
respiratory problems	Bernadine of Sienna
ruptures, against	Drogo; Florentius of Strasburg; Osmund

S

scrofulous diseases	Balbina; Marculf; Mark the Evangelist
skin disease	Anthony the Abbot; George; Marculf; Peregrine Laziosi; Roch (Rocco)
skin rashes	Anthony the Abbot; George; Marculf; Peregrine Laziosi; Roch (Rocco)
sleepwalkers, sleepwalking	Dymphna
smallpox	Matthias
snakebite victims	Hilary; Paul

spasms	John the Baptist
sterility, against	Agatha; Anne; Anthony of Padua; Casilda of Toledo; Felicity; Fiacre; Francis of Paola; Giles; Henry II; Margaret of Antioch; Medard; Philomena; Rita of Cascia; Theobald Roggeri
stillborn children	Edmund
stomach disease, stomach trouble	Brice; Charles Borromeo; Erasmus; Timothy; Wolfgang
stroke	Andrew Avellino; Wolfgang
struma	Balbina; Marculf; Mark the Evangelist
surgery patients	Infant of Prague
syphilis	Fiacre; George; Symphoroian of Autun

T

throat diseases, against	Andrew the Apostle; Blaise; Etheldreda; Godelieve; Ignatius of Antioch; Lucy of Syracuse; Swithbert
toothaches	Apollonia; Chirstopher; Elizabeth of Hungary; Ida of Nivelles; Kea; Medard; Osmund
tuberculosis	Pantaleon; Theresa of Liseaux
twitching, against	Bartholomew the Apostle; Cornelius
typhus, against; against typhoid	Adelard

U

ulcers, against	Charles Borromeo; Job

V

venereal disease	Fiacre
verbal spousal abuse	Anne Marie Taigi; Godelieve; Monica

vertigo, against	Ulric

W

whooping cough, against	Blaise; Winoc
women in labor	Anne; Erasmus; John of Bridlington; Margaret (or Marina) of Antioch; Margaret of Fontana; Mary of Oignies
women who wish to be mothers	Andrew the Apostle
wounds	Aldegundis; Marciana; Rita of Cascia

Handbook for Ministers of Care

Paperback, 6 x 9, 96 pages
978-1-56854-102-0
Order code: HBMCR2 **$8**

GENEVIEVE GLEN, OSB, MARILYN KOFLER, SP, AND KEVIN E. O'CONNOR ■ This is a manual for those already involved in the ministry of care, and for those preparing to undertake this vital work. In these pages you will learn a theology of sickness and suffering, how the Communion ritual works, practical advice on making pastoral visits, how to take care of yourself while caring for others, and where to find further information about illnesses affecting those you visit.

AWARDS:

Catholic Press Association 1998 Book Award winner, first place, in pastoral ministry

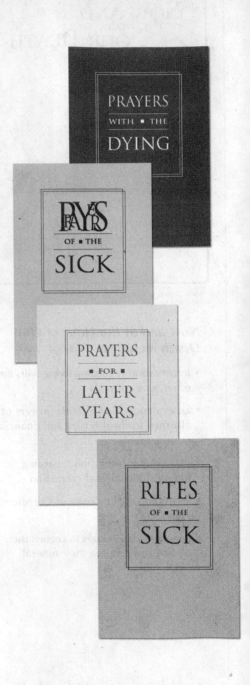